Welcome...

Everyone knows something about Photoshop. For some it will be little more than the name. Others will understand that it's used in the production of pretty much every professionally-produced newspaper and magazines around the world, somewhere along the line. Others will have experienced first hand the power of its advanced tools, and understand the radical difference it can make to anything from a mundane holiday snap to a campaign-winning political poster.

We live in a visual world, and we're bombarded from all sides by pictures designed to sell us something – either a physical product or an ideology. Without Photoshop, the job of those salespeople would be far harder. It's not an exaggeration to say, therefore, that Photoshop may be the most influential application ever in the history of modern computing.

In this guide we'll look at how you can join them, and use the power of

Photoshop to improve your own pictures. We'll walk you through the most compelling features and show you how you can pick the right tool for any job, tweak the way it works, and put it to use in your day-to-day image editing.

We've approached the subject from the point of view of an absolute beginner, so we don't expect you to have any previous experience of using the software. We have also written it with both Windows and Mac users in mind, so whichever platform

you're using you'll find all the information you need to get started right away.

Learning to use a new application can feel like a daunting prospect, but approach Photoshop with an open mind and you'll find that it's actually a lot of fun. You'll be learning by playing with your photos, and rather than ending up with a dry spreadsheet or a letter to your bank, you'll be knocking your pictures into shape. By the end, you may just want to find some space for them on your walls...

Photoshop for Beginners

WRITTEN BY Nik Rawlinson

DENNIS PUBLISHING LTD
GROUP MANAGING DIRECTOR · Ian Westwood
MANAGING DIRECTOR · John Garewal
MD OF ADVERTISING · Julian Lloyd-Evans
NEWSTRADE DIRECTOR · David Barker
CHIEF OPERATING OFFICER · Brett Reynolds
GROUP FINANCE DIRECTOR · Ian Leggett
CHIEF EXECUTIVE · James Tye
CHAIRMAN · Felix Dennis

PUBLISHING AND MARKETING
MAGBOOK PUBLISHER · Dharmesh Mistry · 020 7907 6100
MARKETING EXECUTIVE · Paul Goodhead · 020 7907 6012

LIABILITY

While every care was taken during the production of this MagBook, the publishers cannot be
held responsible for the accuracy of the information or any consequences arising from it.
Dennis Publishing takes no responsibility for the companies advertising in this MagBook.

The paper used in this magazine is produced from sustainable fibre,
manufactured with a valid chain of custody.

Contents

Before we begin...

Photoshop runs on both the Mac and the PC. On each platform they share a common interface. The panels look very similar, the tools work in an identical manner, the files they create can be opened on either platform without issue, and the menus contain the same options in the same positions.

However, in one respect, the Mac and Windows platforms differ significantly, and that's where keyboard shortcuts are concerned.

Rival keyboard layouts

On the Mac, most shortcuts make use of the 'command' key. There are two of these; one either side of the space bar. To open a new document, therefore, a Mac user would press command-n. The shortcut to save it would be command-s.

Windows users, who don't have a command key, would more often use control, with the two options mentioned above defaulting to the shortcuts control-n and control-s. Although Macs have a control

key, too, it's not used in this manner. Neither can Mac users employ the alt key to pull down menus, so while alt-f would open the file menu on Windows it wouldn't do anything of the sort on the Mac.

A further confusion can be caused by the very name of this key. Recent Mac keyboards mark this button 'alt', but older ones call it 'option' (some sport both names). Some software, including some produced by Apple, still uses 'option' to describe this key, even though recent converts to the platform may find this confusing.

This guide is designed to be read by both Windows and Mac users. We shall therefore avoid using keyboard shortcuts that are specific to just one platform. Where shortcuts are

used, we will explain how they are employed on both Windows and the Mac, but wherever possible we will work through menus pulled down using the mouse.

Mouse conventions

Pretty much every mouse connected to a Windows PC has two buttons, usually configured so that the left button performs the primary selection and clicking function, while the right button calls up context sensitive menus that change depending on what you're clicking.

Although two-buttoned mice work in the same manner on a Mac, fewer Mac users have one. If you're using an Apple Mighty Mouse or Magic Mouse

APPLE MAGIC MOUSE

and haven't changed the way it works you will have only one button available to you. When we talk about right-clicking, therefore, you should hold the control button and click the mouse as usual. The result will be the same as it would have been if you had been using a two-buttoned mouse.

If you have swapped the operation of your mouse buttons on either platform to take account of using the mouse in your left hand, when we talk about clicking an on-screen element, then use whichever button you have set up as the primary controller on your device, and when we talk about right-clicking, use the secondary button, irrespective of their positions in your hand.

Photoshop interface

We will be taking the screen grabs throughout this book on a Mac, but Adobe's unified interface looks almost identical on the PC, and so Windows users should have no difficulty in finding their way around their own particular installation with reference to these images.

We shall also be using the latest version of Photoshop. At the time of writing that would be Photoshop CS6. Although, as we will explain in the buying choices section, this includes many new features that are not present in previous versions of Photoshop, much of what we cover here will be just as relevant to CS5.5 and earlier. Where possible, we will make it clear if a particular feature we are covering is not applicable to earlier releases.

If you don't have your own copy Photoshop CS6 and would like to follow along with this book, then you can download a trial version from *adobe.com/downloads*. This will work for 30 days before it needs to be activated, at which point you can either buy a copy or walk away without incurring any further charge.

Chapter 1
Introducing Photoshop

Photoshop is ubiquitous. It's recognised by loyal fans the world over as the most powerful and flexible image editing tool available on any platform. It's name has even become a byword for image editing. How many times have you heard someone claim that an image in print or online has been 'Photoshopped'?

•

If you're just starting out with Photoshop then you have plenty to learn, but there's a lot of fun ahead, too. So, gather together a folder of your favourite photos and get ready to explore the power and creativity afforded by this remarkable app.

•

In this chapter we'll show you how to set up Photoshop to work the way you need it to, and walk you through key interface elements.

Which Photoshop is right for you?

Photoshop is just Photoshop, right? There's no confusion, and no choice to be made... Well no, actually, not quite.

Although the full-blown Photoshop is one of the best-known tools for any job on any platform – easily ranking alongside the likes of Word and Excel, the name can, and does, apply to a whole family of image editing applications.

In this book we'll concern ourselves primarily with the long-standing and full-featured Photoshop app – specifically the CS6 edition, which at the time of writing is the most recent release.

Before we get started, though, it's important to make sure that this is indeed the right tool for you, so in this section we'll take a walk through the various members of the Photoshop family to make sure that you've chosen – or are about to buy – the best app to suit your needs.

Photoshop CS6

Photoshop CS6 is a monster of an application. It's extremely powerful, and its abilities are all too easy to underestimate. Most people will use it only to dabble with their photos, but as well as lightening dark skies and toning down any over exposed parts of your picture it's ripe for applying special effects and adjustments with a single click, working with vector artwork that previously would have been possible only with the help of a dedicated tool like Adobe Illustrator, has a built-in media management tool in the form of Adobe Bridge and lets you output your work in a range of formats suitable for use in print and online.

The Photoshop file format is still controlled by Adobe, but it has become something of an industry standard, and so support from third-party manufacturers and developers is widespread and growing.

The CS6 upgrade introduces new content-aware tools that make it easy to move elements

---

Quick reference: Which Photoshop?

Adobe Photoshop CS6
Standard image editing tool for general use with adjustments and comping tools, and flexible output options.

Adobe Photoshop CS6 Extended
As above, but with additional 3D functions and analytical tools

Adobe Photoshop Lightroom 4
Dedicated to photography and RAW file editing, largely concerning itself with frame-wide edits

Adobe Photoshop Elements 11
Beginners' and home users' edition with neat creativity tools, but missing the most compelling features of the full version

---

» *Photoshop CS6 has adopted the dark interface first used in Photoshop Lightroom, and in CS6 also uses the reversed crop tool that quickly starts to feel a lot more logical than it did in its previous incarnation.*

within your image and rely on Photoshop to fill in the gaps they might leave behind. The underlying graphics engines have been upgraded so it runs more quickly. The crop tool has been completely reengineered so that it now works in the opposite direction to the way that it did in CS5.5 and earlier, but in a manner that matches the crop tool in Lightroom, which makes it easy for those who use both applications to switch between them.

Photoshop CS6 has a new oil painting filter, brushes that erode as you use them for more realistic painting results, the ability to highlight and search layers in your document, 64-bit support for lighting effects and an intuitive video creation process. In short, Adobe has thrown in a whole load of new features to encourage an update, and it certainly feels like a more worthwhile investment than the move from CS5 to CS5.5.

Photoshop CS6 Extended

Photoshop CS6 Extended features all of the tools that appear in the regular edition, but enhances them with 3D image editing including control over shadows, lights, materials, and paints. You can easily incorporate 3D objects in your photos and paint directly onto 3D models.

It also has a range of analysis tools, but unless you're a 3D artist and you want to be able

» *Photoshop Lightroom is aimed squarely at photographers, putting photo management square and centre, with advanced tools allowing you to make significant frame-wide changes by dragging sliders.*

to incorporate your work into a Photoshop document, it's likely that you'll find most of what you need is in the standard edition.

Photoshop Lightroom 4

Photoshop Lightroom 4 is a very different proposition altogether. Although an Adobe application, and although it still carries the Photoshop brand, it is developed in a completely different place and built for subtly different audience. As its name suggests, it's aimed at professional photographers who in the days of film and paper would have spent their time working in a dark room.

Many of these traditional photographers would have applied their edits across the whole frame at once, with a negative exposed for longer or shorter periods of time depending on the effect they wanted to have on the light-sensitive paper.

Other tools such as dodging and burning would allow them to make subtle adjustments to specific parts of the image, but on the whole they would be looking to produce a balanced result that was an accurate reflection of the original scene rather than composing a collage of disparate parts as many creative artists do today using Photoshop CS6 and its predecessors.

Lightroom, then, and the way in which you use it, brings up to date this old way of working. Most of the edits that you apply in Lightroom will be applied across the whole frame in one sweep by dragging sliders in the Lightroom interface and changing the values of various settings such as the strength of shadows, the saturation of colours and the level of clarity in the image.

However, just as traditional photographers are able to dodge and burn specific parts of the frame, so Lightroom users can employ a series of brushes and gradients to apply changes to just parts of their image and make minor, localised lighting and colour corrections rather than specific additions and subtractions.

With this in mind, unless you're a professional photographer who wants both an efficient tool for cataloguing their work and an efficient editing environment that works on a largely frame-wide basis, the traditional Photoshop application is more likely to remain a better bet. For photographers, though, Lightroom is hard to beat, and because it can share data with photo shop you can use the two side-by-side and open up unlimited creative possibilities.

Photoshop Elements 11

Photoshop Elements is a trimmed down version of the full Photoshop application, which is designed to be used by less demanding users, who will often be working on their images at home and in their leisure time. In this respect it is considerably cheaper than the full edition and includes many features that aren't found in Photoshop CS6.

For example, Elements' Photomerge tool lets you bring together the best parts of several different images to create a single perfect shot, such as a group portrait in which the faces of each person are drawn from different images, depending on which one was the most flattering representation of each subject.

» *Photoshop Elements is a low-cost entry point to the Photoshop family, but although it has some compelling offerings it lacks many core features of Photoshop CS6.*

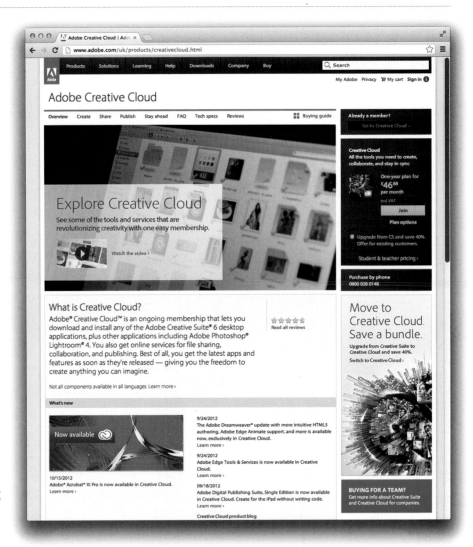

Other one-click tools let you whiten people's teeth and make the sky more appealing. It has scrapbooking tools and creative options for producing calendars, cards and so on, and you can output your work not only for print and the web, but also as an interactive movie.

However, Elements is missing many important features. For example, it has less extensive support for exporting different file types, can't work with 3D, has fewer image processing tools, no dedicated option for recovering shadows and highlights, and leaves you much more limited when it comes to painting tools.

For anyone creating graphics for the web to use on their own site, or who wants to improve their holiday photography in post production before sharing it with family and friends, Photoshop Elements is a great choice. It's also something of a bargain. However, it limits your creativity and flexibility, and in that respect the more expensive Photoshop CS6 remains the better bet.

» *Signing up to Creative Cloud means you'll benefit from upgrades on a more frequent basis, and can spread the cost over time.*

How to buy Photoshop

Traditionally there was only one way to buy Photoshop, and that was as a boxed standalone product. You can still do that, but as Adobe has added more and more related applications to its portfolio, such as Dreamweaver for web design, InDesign for professional page layout, Illustrator for working with vector graphics, and so on, it has increasingly sold Photoshop as part of its Creative Suite bundle, which includes a range of other tools.

Precisely what that range is depends, as Adobe sells a variety of different Creative Suite bundles. For example, those who work predominantly with print might want to buy Creative Suite Design Standard, which includes Photoshop, Illustrator, InDesign, Acrobat, Bridge and Media Encoder. Those who work on the web, meanwhile, would more likely be interested in Design and Web Premium, which adds Flash, Fireworks and Dreamweaver into the mix. There are other bundles for those who work predominantly with video, and the Master Collection, which includes all of the applications in one box.

If you need two or more apps it is often cheaper to buy a Creative Suite bundle than to pay for each one individually.

However, with the introduction of CS6, Adobe debuted a new option for buying its software, and that is a monthly or yearly software subscription service called Creative Cloud.

Creative Cloud gives you access to all of the applications in the Master Collection for an ongoing monthly fee. You can either sign up for a single month at a slightly higher price or a year – a deal that attracts a discount.

Throughout the length of your subscription Adobe will continue to develop and release updates for each application, and these will be available to download immediately, so you won't have too wait a year to 18 months for Adobe to release a new boxed product before you can feel the benefit. Better yet, when Adobe releases a new version of Creative Suite – such as CS6.5 or CS7 when it eventually appears – your subscription will roll on and you'll be able to download the new edition.

For anyone who uses several applications and prefers to always be running the most up-to-date version either because they like using the new tools or because they need to remain compatible with clients and colleagues, a Creative Cloud subscription will likely work out to be a cheaper way to buy in to the Adobe applications.

Although you can buy boxed versions both of the individual apps and Creative Suite from third parties like Amazon and regular retailers, and you can download apps like Photoshop Elements from digital stores like the Mac App Store, you can only sign up to a Creative Cloud subscription through Adobe's website at adobe.com. Naturally, you'll need to maintain an active Internet connection and a valid credit card for the duration of your membership, as you'll be charged recurring payments and your computer will check in with Adobe's servers from time to time to make sure that its subscription is still valid.

Teachers, students and education pricing

Adobe offers generous discounts for those who are students or employed in the education sector. These can run to as much as 80% and are valid on both Creative Cloud and regular downloaded or boxed product editions of the company's software. Check out the dedicated education pricing pages on the Adobe website.

How did we get here? Photoshop through the ages

Photoshop's history is just as long and distinguished, as it is clearly recorded. It all began in 1987, when Thomas Knoll who at the time was a student at the University of Michigan, wrote an application called Display. By modern standards it was fairly conservative, designed only to show greyscale images on the monochrome monitor of his Macintosh Plus.

However, even such humble beginnings were fairly radical in their day, and when Knoll' brother, John, saw what Thomas was working on, he immediately grasped its potential. John Knoll worked at Industrial Light and Magic, the film graphics company responsible for the original Star Wars movies and is now owned by Disney.

Jon wanted to see Display go further, and encouraged Thomas to extend its features set into full-on image editing. Photoshop's seeds were sown.

The early years

Thomas and John Knoll worked on Display together and finally settled on the name Photoshop in 1998. They sold 200 copies by bundling it with scanners. However, John also demonstrated what it could do to both Apple and Adobe, and Adobe signed up to license and distribute the product. Two years later, in 1990, Photoshop 1.0 shipped. It was available only on the Mac.

Photoshop finally appeared on Windows when it hit version 2.5, in November 1992. By that point it could work with the standard four colours used in print production: cyan, magenta, yellow and black, mixing them in varying degrees to produce other tones. It supported paths, too, and a year later also appeared on the Solaris and IRIX platforms, although these were dropped after version 3 shipped in November 1994.

Photoshop's development has been steady and impressive ever since. Version 3 introduced the concept of layers, which allow you to build up an image with different elements above and below those that surround them. Effects can be applied

The Knoll brothers: Where are they now?

Thomas Knoll continues to work on the development of Photoshop. He was the lead developer on the project as recently as the release of Photoshop CS4. He now spends his time working on the Camera RAW plug-in that allows Photoshop to work with data drawn down directly from digital cameras' sensors without prior conversion.

His brother John still works at Industrial Light and Magic. His work can be seen on the Star Wars prequel movies, as well as the late 1990s re-releases of the three original films. Outside of the Star Wars universe, he is also credited with work on Pirates of the Caribbean, Harry Potter and Mission Impossible.

Photoshop Codenames

Like many software companies, Adobe uses codenames when developing its applications. Several of these have become common knowledge thanks to their use in relased 'beta' (development) builds of the application, including:

- *Fast Eddy* – Photoshop 2, June 1991
- *Big Electric Cat* – Photoshop 4, November 1996
- *Strange Cargo* – used for both Photoshop 5 and Photoshop 5.5 in may 1998 and February 1999 respectively
- *Dark Matter* – the first Creative Suite edition of Photoshop, released in October 2003
- *Superstition* – Photoshop CS6, May 2012

just a certain layers, so editing one doesn't commit changes to the image as a whole.

Version 4, which was the first edition released simultaneously on Windows and the Mac, built on the support for layers with adjustment layers, which let

you apply adjustments to those elements stacked below them and adjust the strength of the adjustment by changing that layer's opacity.

By version 5 we could work with editable type, had a history palette that let us undo

multiple actions, and were introduced to the magnetic lasso which made it easier to trim out parts of an image and work on them in isolation or remove them altogether.

Photoshop enter the new millennium with version 6, codenamed Venus in Furs, which shipped in September 2000. This saw the arrival of the liquify filter, vector shapes and a new interface, which has been redesigned again since then to reflect the interface design developed for Photoshop Lightroom.

After that came the last edition of photo shop that did not carry the Creative Suite branding. Photoshop 7 debuted one of the most radical tools in its arsenal: the Healing Brush. This seemingly magical tool took all of the paint out of fixing imperfections in your photos by allowing you to

» *Adobe Camera Raw lets you open native camera sensor data in Photoshop so that you have a richer, more flexible file on which to perform your edits.*

» *The Photoshop interface has evolved slowly through most of its editions. This is Photoshop CS3, which sports the then well-known light interface, which has since been replaced by a dark, unified window.*

simply paint over the problem area and leave Photoshop to remove the blemish and patch over the selected area by sampling its surroundings. It worked pretty well for a first release, and has only ever improved over time.

The birth of Creative Suite

In 2003, Adobe dropped the idea of individual application version numbers and started to think in terms of suites. Adobe

Creative Suite appeared in October, along with Photoshop CS and a host of CS brethren.

Adobe marked the move by shipping a bumper upgrade, packed with new features. Chief among them was a new RAW processing tool used to work directly with the raw data pulled from a camera's sensor when it writes a file to the memory card. The version in Photoshop was RAW 2; the first release was an add-on to Photoshop 7, so it was

really only a tweak. However, Photoshop CS, then, marked the first major advance for photographers in several years.

That wasn't the only improvement, though, as Photoshop CS could now match colours between images so that they looked like they were part of a set, images could now be up to 300,000 pixels in either direction, it could work with files of up to 2GB each and it had smart guides to aid alignment and layout.

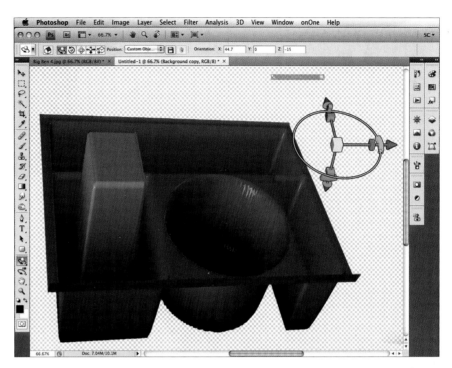

» *Adobe has shipped standard and Extended editions of Photoshop over the last few years, with 3D features in the Extended apps.*

The momentum continued for Photoshop CS2 which again saw a reworking of the Camera RAW feature and the introduction of Smart Objects which embed external elements within a document and automatically formats them to fit the available space, aspect ratio and orientation. It had corrections for lens distortions and redeye, and the Patch tool was joined by a Healing Brush that again pushed users abilities to apply quick fixes without any advanced expertise on their part.

Adobe has built on each of these enhancements over the years until reaching Creative Suite 6. Photoshop CS6 now features the seventh release of the Camera RAW tool, is able to preserve skin tones and detect faces when making edits, has a much improved interface and now understands the contents of the image environment in which it is working, so if you resize an photo or rotate it unevenly, it's able to fill in any gaps that might appear around the edges.

Photoshop and the future

Photoshop is so successful that Adobe simply can't afford not to carry on developing, although second-guessing what it might have in store gets more difficult with every release as any potential gap seems already to have been plugged.

For Windows users, and particularly those on older machines, Adobe has already given warning that it will discontinue support for Windows XP with the next release. Writing on the Adobe Photoshop blog, product manager Tom Hogarty said,

'The Photoshop team would like to provide advanced notice that Photoshop CS6 (13.0) will be the last major version of Photoshop to support Windows XP. (Photoshop CS6 does not support Windows Vista.) In addition, all subsequent Photoshop feature updates specifically for Creative Cloud members will no longer support Windows XP.'

Adobe Photoshop Lightroom already lacked support for Windows XP.

There was no word on how far back the next version of Photoshop would go when supporting Macs and OS X.

Fundamentals of the Photoshop CS6 interface

The Photoshop interface now looks radically different to its appearance in previous versions, as it has aligned itself with the darker design language used for Photoshop Lightroom. However, many principles employed in previous version still apply here.

01   The drop-down menus largely open up image-wide options controlling the way that Photoshop works, including image size and resolution, canvas size and colour space.

02   The bar across the top of the interface is context-sensitive and centralises the options that apply to the currently selected tool.

03   Control the layout of the Photoshop interface by picking from common workspace configurations for specific tasks or saving your favoured layouts so that you can quickly call them up again in the future.

04   Holding down on tools whose icons bear a small triangle in the lower right corner opens a fly-out menu containing supplementary options or related tools.

05   As with the extended tool panels, holding down on a collapsed panel opens it up temporarily. Clicking the two chevrons at the top of this columns opens it up to its full width.

06   The Layers panel is one of the most important parts of Photoshop, and one that you will return to frequently throughout your time in the application. Dragging layers up and down within this palette changes their stacking.

Quick reference: Photoshop tools

You'll find many of Photoshop's most compelling features in its menus, or organised in palettes, but your key creative tools still reside in the tool bar. Most often this is anchored to the left of the application window, but you can drag it to any position on your display by holding the dotted line above the tools themselves.

You can show and hide the toolbox by picking Window | Tools, and change it from a tall column just a single tool wide to a double width panel like the one to the right.

Notice how many of the tools have a small triangle in the lower right corner. This signifies a hidden menu. Clicking the tool once selects the mode indicated by its icon, but holding down calls up the menu and changes the icon to whichever option you select from the menu. Because these changed icons can make the toolbar look unfamiliar we have reproduced all of the fly-out menus to the right for easy reference.

Tools in brief

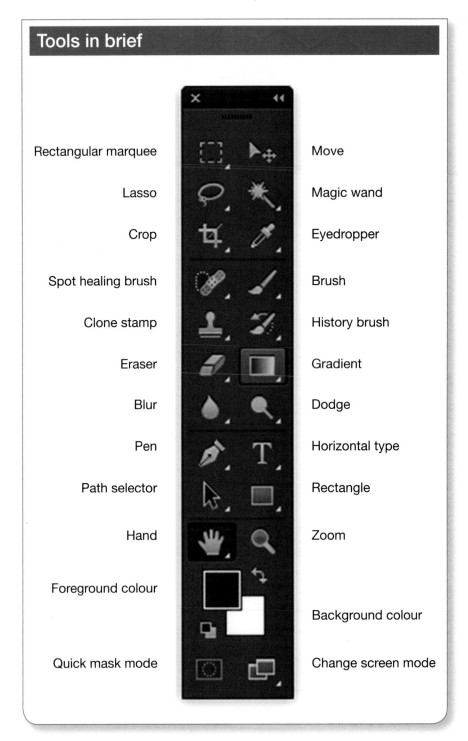

Rectangular marquee — Move

Lasso — Magic wand

Crop — Eyedropper

Spot healing brush — Brush

Clone stamp — History brush

Eraser — Gradient

Blur — Dodge

Pen — Horizontal type

Path selector — Rectangle

Hand — Zoom

Foreground colour

Background colour

Quick mask mode — Change screen mode

Marquee tool

Used to select areas on the canvas by dragging with the mouse. Shortcut M. The fly-out menu gives you access to selection areas of different shapes.

Lassoo tool

Select freeform areas by drawing outlines. Polygonal Lasso works with straight lines; Magnetic Lasso detects contrasts and sticks to them to aid cutting out objects. Shortcut L.

Crop tool

Trims the image to specified sizes. Shortcut C. Slice tools are used to split the image so that it can be selectively compressed and recomposed in a web page. Perspective Crop Tool isolated regular objects taken from an angle.

Spot healing brush tool

Lets you paint over parts of your image and have their contents replaced by textures automatically generated by Photoshop with reference to the area's surroundings. Shortcut J. Also used to correct red eye in photos.

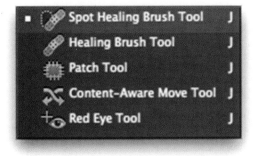

Clone stamp tool

Lets you copy content from one area to another by sampling the reference and painting over another section. Shortcut S. Pattern stamp, as its name suggests, does the same with patterns.

Eraser tool

As its name suggests, it erases parts of the image. Shortcut E. Background Eraser removes areas of similar colour surrounding a subject, while Magic Eraser removes complete areas of contiguous colour with a single click.

Blur / Sharpen / Smudge tool

Three distinct tools that either smooth or sharpen selective areas of an image, rather than the whole canvas as would happen if you used the equivalent tools in the Filter menu. Smudge is useful when working with paint media.

Pen tool

The pen (shortcut P) draws paths to which you can apply a stroke or along which you can run text. The regular pen tool works with Bezier curves, while the Freeform Pen tool lets you draw on the canvas directly. Paths are vector-based.

Path selection tool

Lets you select a path with a single click inside its boundary. The Direct Selection tool is more discrete, expecting you to click the actual path itself, so may be more precise.

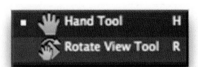

Hand tool

For dragging a layer on the canvas (shortcut H) or rotating the canvas (shortcut R) without using Transform.

Quick Selection tool

Quick selection lets you paint over areas in your image, and have Photoshop select all contiguous areas of the same colour. Magic wand does the same with a single click.

Eyedropper tool

Various tools for selecting colours, measuring, adding notes, counting items in an image or sampling media on a 3D object. Some of these functions, such as 3D sampling and object counting, are only available in Photoshop Extended.

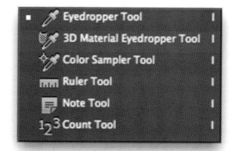

Brush tool

Various tools for directly painting onto the canvas. Shortcut B. Colour replacement tool lets you paint over existing colours with new ones, without straying beyond the edges. The Mixer Brush smears adjacent colours naturally.

History brush tool

A smart tool that selectively rolls back the portion of the image that you paint over to previous states. Shortcut Y.

Bucket tools

Various ways of filling the canvas with either continuous colour (Paint Bucket) or a graduating tint from one colour to another or opaque to transparent (Gradient tool). 3D Material Drop quickly applies surfaces to 3D objects.

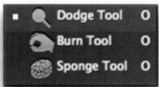

Dodge, burn and sponge

Three tools that emulate traditional photographic tools. Dodge lightens an area by reducing the strength of the content on the selected later in that area. Burn does the opposite. Sponge increases the saturation of an area.

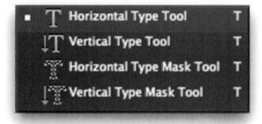

Type tools

Loads the type engine for directly entering text horizontally or vertically. The type mask tools apply the text outlines as a selection that you can use to define which areas of the underlying image remain visible.

Vector graphics tools

Photoshop can now handle vector graphics better than ever before. Each graphic is positioned on its own layer to keep them separate from your bitmap artwork. Flexible options on the status bar at the top of the interface let you define their border and fill colour, the width and style of the border, how they align with other objects and their pixel perfect proportions.

Screen mode options

Most of the time you'll want to run Photoshop with all of the regular palettes and toolbars in view for easy access. However, if you're running on a smaller monitor or you want to view your work without distraction you can change that here. Pressing tab and temporarily hides all toolbars and palettes.

Choosing, changing and working with colours

Colours and light are fundamental to the creation of visual art. Without light we would have only a black canvas; without colours we could only work in greyscale. Successful artwork requires a careful balance of the two.

Photoshop has a flexible, intuitive colour engine that controls both the colour space in which you're working, and the colours you're using.

RGB vs CMYK

If you're working with images you have downloaded from your digital camera, they'll almost certainly be encoded within the RGB colour space (see the definition box, above right) where each pixel in the frame is defined according to the amount of red, green or blue that must be mixed together to result in that tone.

If you want to incorporate the results of your editing work in a magazine or book to be printed by a professional press, then you'll almost certainly

need to convert it to the CMYK colour space so that it contains all of the data required to direct the correct amounts of the cyan, magenta, yellow and black ink used by printers onto the page to reproduce the image.

This is simple, as Photoshop lets you switch between different colour space models by picking them from the Image | Mode menu (see right).

The option to switch between 8, 16 or 32 bits per channel defines how fine-grained the colour definitions

will be. The higher this number, the greater fidelity of your finished work will be since Photoshop will be able to call on a broader number of tones when building the image.

Quick definition: What is a colour space?

Colour spaces are abstract concepts. They describe the primary colours that are mixed together to create all other tones. In the real world we often talk about red, yellow and blue being the primary colours from which you can make all other tones. However, in design we more often consider red, green, blue (RGB) or cyan, magenta, yellow, black (CYMK) for screen and print-based output respectively. We use K for black, rather than B, so that it's bot confused with the B for Blue in RGB.

By mixing R, G and B in differing quantities within the RGB *colour space* we can theoretically create any tone that the display in question is capable of producing. By doing the same with different quantities of C, M, Y and K on paper we can emulate those tones on paper.

How to use the Photoshop colour picker

Click to select a tone directly. Drag to see the preview update dynamically in the colour chip to the right.

Click within this strip or drag your mouse up and down to change the part of the colour spectrum displayed in the main picker area.

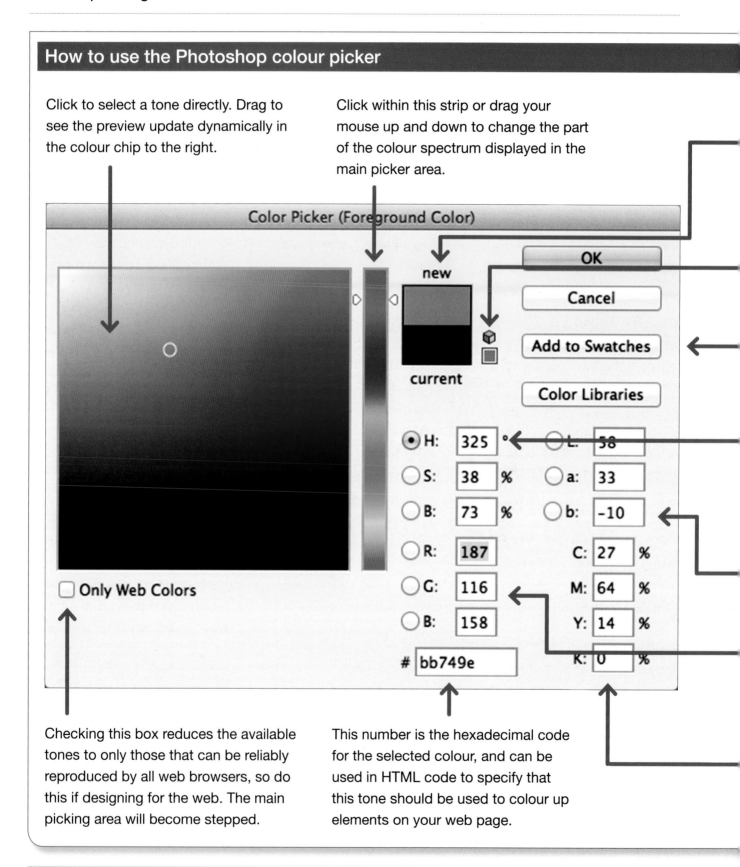

Color Picker (Foreground Color)

new

current

OK

Cancel

Add to Swatches

Color Libraries

H: 325 °
S: 38 %
B: 73 %
R: 187
G: 116
B: 158

L: 58
a: 33
b: -10
C: 27 %
M: 64 %
Y: 14 %
K: 0 %

bb749e

☐ Only Web Colors

Checking this box reduces the available tones to only those that can be reliably reproduced by all web browsers, so do this if designing for the web. The main picking area will become stepped.

This number is the hexadecimal code for the selected colour, and can be used in HTML code to specify that this tone should be used to colour up elements on your web page.

The colour chip shows the difference between the tone you have clicked in the picker (at the top) and the current tone in use (bottom). This lets you see how they might compliment or clash with each other before committing yourself.

Click the box below the cube to automatically pick the closest web-safe equivalent to the tone you have selected in the main colour choosing box to the left.

Click the Add to Swatches button to save the colour you have selected to the Swatches palette so that you can easily find it again in the future. If it's not currently visible, you can display this palette by picking it from the Window menu.

HSB stands for hue, saturation, brightness. Hue describes the tone itself, saturation is its strength and brightness is, logically, how bright it is. As with all of these boxed sections, you can type in values to change the cursor's position in the picker.

The Lab colour space used values for lightness (L), the and the mix of colours on a scale of green to magenta (a) and blue to yellow (b). It is said that the Lab colour space more accurately reproduces the field of vision of the human eye.

RGB lets you specify the relative quantities of red, green and blue that are used to create a particular tone. This colourspace is the one used by the vast majority of computers monitors, televisions, digital cameras and scanners.

CMYK is used by printers – both home inkjets and commercial printing companies – to specify how different values of cyan, magenta, yellow and black inks should be mixed to reproduce your chosen tones on paper.

Colours and the web

Although it's becoming less critical with the growing abilities of modern computers, tablets and browsers, it once paid dividends to be very careful when picking colours for use on the web.

Different devices using slight different colours models, and so the only way to be sure that the colours you used in your work would look the same on every screen was to restrict yourself to a narrow palette of 216 tones that could reliably be displayed on any device.

That's less often the case today, but if you want to be sure of having the greatest possible chance of producing work that will look the same in your viewers' browsers as it does in your own, check the Only Web Colours option to restrict the number of tones from which you can choose.

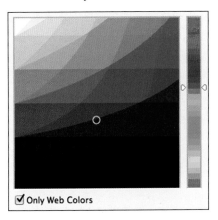

Only Web Colors

Sampling colours with the Eyedropper

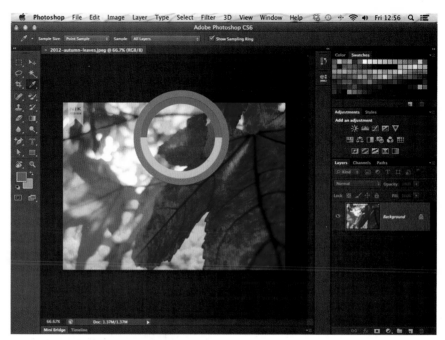

» *The Eyedropper tool lets you sample colour from one or more layers so you can ensure greater consistency throughout your designs.*

You'll frequently find yourself wanting to re-use colours that have already appeared elsewhere in your image to ensure consistency throughout your work. The easiest way to do this is with the eyedropper tool. Select it from the tools palette (see the icon above), or use the shortcut 'I'. This has several different modes, so keep tapping I until you get to the icon above, or select Eyedropper Tool from the flyout menu on that icon where it sits on the toolbar.

In its default state, the Eyedropper Tool samples the exact colour of the pixel you click and uses that to change the current foreground colour.

However, with a few simple tweaks you can quickly change this to work in a more flexible manner.

Using the Eyedropper to change the background

Hold the Alt key before you start clicking on the canvas and the colour selection will be applied to the background rather than the foreground colour. You can continue to drag around the canvas with alt held down to change the colour of the background on the fly (just as you can drag with the mouse held down to change the foreground on the fly) until you reach the exact tone you're after.

Changing the sample size

Because your eyes are unlikely to be able to make out each individual pixel on your screen, the colours they see on the canvas are more often made up from a range of different tones

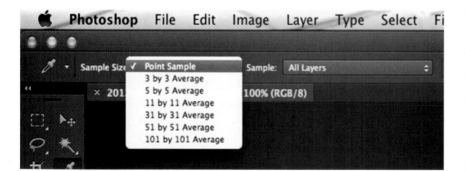

positioned very close to one another on the display. Picking just one pixel from among them might therefore not result in a foreground or background colour that looks anything like the overall tone in front of you.

To more accurately replicate the general colour, therefore, you need to change the sample size, and task Photoshop with picking a colour that is an average of each of the sampled tones within that area.

Do this on the toolbar (see below) by picking anything up to 101 by 101 pixels square. The result will automatically be a complimentary tone that works with each of the pixels in the bounding zone.

Colour sampler

The Colour Sampler is closely related to the Eyedropper tool, but is used for information gathering rather than setting colours. It's selected from the same fly-out menu as the Eyedropper, or you can repeatedly press the 'I' key until you cycle through to the

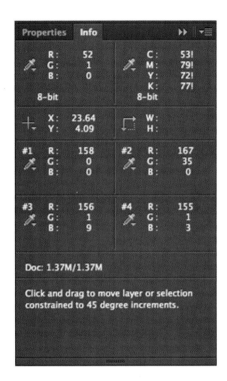

Colour Sampler tool (see icon, left) which lets you drop up to four reference points onto your image, with the colour values of the tones found at those points displayed in the document Info palette (see above).

You can change the colour space for the first two sets of displayed values, and use them as references when you are picking new colours, and retrieve them when you next open the file as they are saved along with the document data if you use Photoshop file formats.

Colour palettes

If you frequently need to make changes to your foreground and background colours, bring the color and swatches palettes into play. You'll find them on the Window menu (see below).

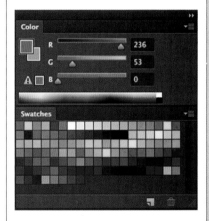

The Color panel lets you drag sliders or enter values to mix your colours without using the full colour dialogue. It includes a web safe chip to pick the closest web safe colour to your current tone.

The Swatches panel contains all of your saved colours, including the ones set automatically by Photoshop. You can store new swatches in this panel by clicking the new document icon on its bottom border, and delete them with the trash icon.

How to set up Photoshop for the first time

Photoshop is ready to use as soon as you unbox or download it. However, a few tweaks here and there can make a big difference to its efficiency and the way you spend your working time in the application.

Here we'll walk you through the Preferences panels that control how Photoshop works on your particular machine. You can find this on the Windows edition at the bottom of the Edit menu, and on the Mac by clicking the Photoshop application name on the top-of-screen menubar.

A word about activation

To use Photoshop for longer than 30 days you'll need to activate it. Make sure you have a live internet connection and then click the button to activate from the application splash screen. To complete activation you'll need to enter the serial number on the packaging, or which you'll have received by email, plus your email address.

01 Use the various options in the channel on the left of the Preferences panel to switch between the various screens.

Your first stop should be the Performance tab through which you can tailor how Photoshop uses your system resources. As with all of the options, if you don't know what you're doing, or how you're likely to spend your time working, leave things as they are. However, if you know what you're doing, consider tweaking the amount of memory that Photoshop is

allowed to address by dragging the slider in the first box.

If you have several hard drives attached to your system, or several partitions on a single disk, and can devote one of these entirely to Photoshop's temporary file storage, specify this in the Scratch Disks section to improve performance.

Finally, if you have the necessary hardware, ensure that the Use Graphics Process box is checked in the fourth pane of the panel to offload some of the processing work.

02 The Units and Rulers settings will be of most interest to print designers. Photoshop is metric, preferring to work in centimetres and points, but if your layouts are specified in inches, perhaps because you're resizing photos to fit in traditional frames, change that here. Also use these options to set resolutions for both screen and print that match your output device. The default settings of 72ppi and 300ppi are correct for most monitors and commercial print operations.

03 The settings for the Camera RAW tool are split off from those for the main Photoshop operations.

The most important consideration here is how you want Photoshop to save the applied image settings. As you'll see in our section on using Camera RAW, when you open a file you have to make certain decisions about how it should be processed, and Photoshop needs to know whether it should save these as part of the file itself or store them externally in a so-called Sidecar file, which is applied to the image every time it is opened. The latter option is often the best solution as it doesn't make any changes to your original photo, but it does mean that you need to make sure the two files – photo and sidecar data – don't get separated at a later date.

Starting work: Getting your photos into Photoshop

Unless you're creating a digital collage from scratch, in which case you'll want to start with a blank canvas, your first task after firing up Photoshop will be to open some assets and get working. As you'll see here, there are several ways you can do that.

The obvious starting point is through the menus by clicking File | Open (or using the shortcut command-o on the Mac or ctrl-o on the PC), which calls up the standard file management dialogue, allowing you to navigate to the folder containing your image, select and load it.

However, it's not quite as dumb as it looks, as there are two supplementary menus at the bottom that you can use to help it access problem files.

Sometimes an image may have corrupted metadata attached, which means that Photoshop can't work out from its file extension, or from the opening few bytes of the file data, what kind of file it is. In this instance you would use the Format drop-down menu to tell it what kind of file it's looking at. It would then use the appropriate import tool to read in the data and display the image. If you need to do this, you should make a habit of immediately saving out a new good copy of the file either in the same format, or an alternative, with the full file name, including its extension, in place.

The menu immediately above this lets you trim down the range of file types displayed in the dialogue above. This way you can quickly zero in on, say, Jpegs or Tiffs and exclude all animated Gifs if you know that

File formats

Photoshop can open and understand a truly boggling array of files, many of which are extremely long in the tooth. As well as various audio and video formats, Photoshop CS6 is happy working with the following still image formats.

- Photoshop PSD
- BMP
- Cineon
- CompuServe GIF
- Photoshop DCS 1.0
- Photoshop DCS 2.0
- DICOM
- Photoshop EPS
- IFF format
- JPEG
- JPEG2000
- OpenEXR
- PCX
- Photoshop PDF

- Pixar
- PNG
- Portable Bit Map
- Photoshop Raw
- Scitex CT
- Targa
- TIFF
- Wireless Bitmap
- Photoshop 2.0 (Mac only)
- PICT (read only)
- PICT Resource (Mac only, can open only)
- Radiance
- Large Document Format PSB

How to navigate the Adobe Bridge interface

Bridge is Adobe's file management tool for Creative Suite. You can use it to quickly find the image you're after and open it in Photoshop. Use the folders (**01**) to open the image location, and scroll through the thumbnails in the central panel (**02**). Clicking a thumbnail opens a larger preview (**03**). If you can't find the image you're after, select criteria from the left-hand column (**04**) to filter down the range of images that are shown in the thumbnail area until you have reduced them to a manageable number. When you have selected an image, you can view its metadata (**05**) below the preview.

» *The Mini Bridge panel that appears at the bottom of the Photoshop interface lets you navigate your folders and open files directly, but relies on you keeping Bridge running in the background.*

the file you're after hasn't been saved in that format.

For more extensive file management you'll need to look to Bridge. This is Adobe's dedicated file navigator, which includes extensive metadata interrogation tools that let you slim down the range of matching files until you have only a handful to manually filter. Check out our orientation box on the previous page to see how it can help you to navigate your files.

There will be times, however, when switching out to Bridge every time you want to open a file is overkill, even if it does speed up the process of finding you assets. At times like this you can instead rely on Mini Bridge, which replicates a subset of the features of the fully-fledged Bridge utility in a panel at the bottom of the Photoshop window. If it's not visible on your machine, click the Mini Bridge tab at the bottom of the screen or activate it through the menus by clicking File | Browse through Mini Bridge...

There are caveats you need to consider here. Specifically, to use Mini Bridge you need to have the full version of Bridge running in the background, which will naturally consume system resources that could otherwise be devoted to use by Photoshop itself. You'll therefore need to make sure that you have a sufficiently well-specced machine if you want to step away from using the regular file management dialogues built in to your operating system (see system specs, right).

Since version 7, Photoshop has also been able to work with RAW data files taken direct from digital camera memory cards.

RAW files are literally a dump of the data produced by the sensor when it samples the incoming light that reaches it through the lens, rather than a Jpeg image that has been created inside the camera by selectively discarding and

System specs

Adobe's stated minimum system requirements for running Photoshop CS6 at the point of writing were:

Mac users
- 64-bit Intel processor
- OS X v10.6.8 or v10.7
- 1GB of memory
- 2GB of hard drive space
- 1024x768 display with 16-bit color and 256MB of VRAM
- OpenGL 2.0–capable system

Windows users
- Intel Pentium 4 or Athlon 64 processor
- Windows XP SP 3, Windows 7 SP 1 or Windows 8
- 1GB of memory
- 1GB of hard drive space
- 1024x768 display with 16-bit color and 256MB of VRAM
- OpenGL 2.0–capable system

Source: http://www.adobe.com/uk/products/photoshop/tech-specs.html

compressing some of the data. The idea is that by working directly with the raw data you will be able to retain a truer representation of the original scene and have more flexible editing options since none of the original data will have been thrown away.

When opening files of this kind Photoshop will invoke the Camera RAW utility, which allows you to specify how the file should be processed before it is rendered as a recognisable image type within the editing environment. This way you can apply certain exposure

corrections such as changing the white balance setting, curve or sharpness of the result.

However, all manufacturers record the data from their sensors in a different manner, and there is often a difference between the data delivered by different cameras from the same manufacturer, which means that not all images can be opened in this way if you don't have the necessary filters. You'll therefore need to keep an eye on available updates and make sure you always download Camera RAW updates when available.

How to use Adobe Camera RAW

Adobe introduced its first raw image processor in February 2003. At the time, the idea of processing data drawn directly from the camera sensor was just taking off as professional-grade applications were starting to be joined by some more affordable options such as Apple Aperture.

With Camera RAW, Adobe made it possible to open this same data in an application that many designers and photographers already used as a key part of their digital workflow: Photoshop.

It is still a key part of Photoshop today, and Adobe regularly updates it so that it can read data from a wider range of cameras. It also uses it as the basis of Photoshop Lightroom, its dedicated processing tool for working with such data and managing and organising large collections of digital images.

The latest version of Camera RAW is 7, which is compatible with Photoshop CS6 and Lightroom 4, but not Photoshop CS5. It has support for over 200 cameras from manufacturers as diverse as Canon, Nikon, Leica and Leaf.

It's important to ensure that you are running the most recent version of Camera RAW so that whichever camera you're using it shouldn't have any trouble reading its native data.

Further, if you prefer to work in this way, it's worth checking whether or not a particular camera is supported before you buy a new one, recognising that it can often take some time for support for a new model to appear within Camera RAW and rival raw processing applications.

Don't be immediately put off if a particular camera isn't supported, though, as Adobe is usually pretty quick when it comes to expanding the range of compatible data formats. In the meantime, you can often set a camera to shoot RAW and JPEG files side by side so that you can enjoy the JPEGs until the necessary RAW processing algorithm is released.

Tech briefing: RAW vs JPEG

So why would you want to shoot RAW images rather than JPEGs? Quite simply, they give you a lot more flexibility once you get them inside Photoshop, and expand your options when it comes to performing an edit.

When your camera creates a JPEG image it's performing a lot of processing itself before writing the result to your memory card. Some of this is to do with fixing the white balance, adjusting the saturation and, crucially, compressing the image so that it takes up less space. It's this last step that is the most destructive as it involves throwing away a lot of the captured data.

If you work with RAW files nothing is thrown away and the camera doesn't apply any formatting changes, leaving you free to apply the processing yourself in an app like Camera RAW.

Camera RAW: What can it do?

Camera RAW lets you make significant improvements to your image before you even touch Photoshop proper. We used it to take this image from its original state (top) to a brighter, puncher version (below) even before it was opened in Photoshop.

Workthrough: Importing images using Camera RAW

Over the next four pages we'll import a RAW camera file using Adobe Camera RAW.

In doing so we will apply a range of adjustments in the RAW processor itself so that by the time we get the image into Photoshop it will already be looking a lot better than the original.

The good news is that while RAW data is more complex than simple JPEGs you don't need to be an expert to make significant changes to the way it looks in its finished form as many of the changes you need to apply are controlled using a simple series of sliders.

Note that you'll only see the Camera RAW processor appear if you try to open a RAW file. Usually you will need to specifically tell your camera to shoot in this manner. You will also need to make sure you're using a compatible file format by checking for your model camera in the list at *adobe.com/ products/photoshop/extend.html*

How to use Camera RAW

Direct selection tools let you drag on the preview image to make changes, rotate the picture, crop it and perform direct adjustments without recourse to the tabbed palette and sliders through which you'll apply most adjustments.

The histogram shows you the strength of each colour at particular light levels, with brighter tones to the right and shadows to the left. Try and keep the highest peaks away from either extremity to avoid losing detail in those areas.

The largest part of the window is given over to a preview of the image. This is an accurate reflection of how the photo will look once you have finished processing it and imported it into Photoshop, so keep working until you're happy with this.

The sliders are your primary tools in Camera RAW. Clicking through the tabs above them opens up a different range on every sheet. Walk through them in a logical, left-to-right manner to make sure you have set each parameter as required.

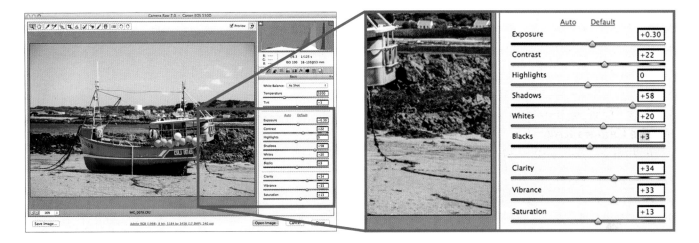

01 Start on the first tab. Often this is the only tab you'll need to use since it handles the primary lighting and colour controls. Here we have slightly increased the exposure, contrast, whites and blacks, and significantly increased the strength of the shadows to give the image more punch. We have also increased the clarity, vibrance and saturation to improve definition.

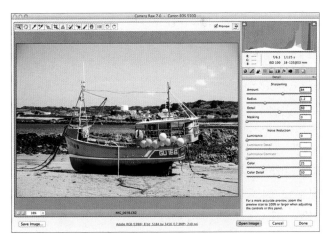

02 We've now moved on to the second tab where we can control the image curves. This gives more fine-grained control over the strength of highlights and shadows in the image. Here we have increased both by dragging the highlights slider higher and the shadows slider lower.

03 Our image is starting to look better already, and could probably be sent to Photoshop now. However, we'll apply a little sharpening to the image so that it looks better on screen. Note that as Camera RAW warns, this is often best performed with the image zoomed to 100%.

04 Camera RAW is a quick and easy way to create a punchy black and white picture. Simply check the Convert to Greyscale box, and you can still use the sliders below it to adjust the balance of the converted tones in the image.

05 Camera RAW doesn't only adjust colours: it can also be used to correct imperfections in the lens on your camera. Here we have applied a barrel distortion correction that has introduced a pincushion effect, so we need to dial it back.

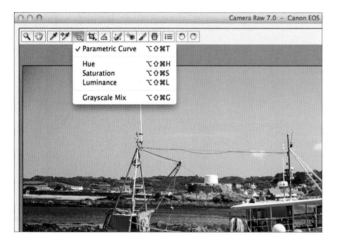

06 If you need to adjust specific colour data for particular parts of the image, select this tool from the toolbar and then click on the area you want to adjust — such as the sky — and drag left and right to tone down or boost the effect.

07 Click Open Image when you have finished working, if you want to write the changes to the file, or hold Alt while clicking to preserve the original file and open a copy. The difference between the raw and edited data is obvious.

Taking things further with Adobe Photoshop Lightroom 4

By now you should have an inkling of the power of the Camera RAW processor, and understand how quickly you can make significant changes to your image just by dragging a few sliders. If you think that this better suits your workflow than a lot of manual editing in Photoshop itself then take a look at Photoshop Lightroom.

Lightroom is built on top of the Camera RAW processor and, although it has a range of selective editing tools such as brushes and gradients, they are only used to control the strength of an effect or direct where it should be applied to the image. They aren't used to build up an image from scratch, and so should be considered similar

to layer masks, but without all of the complexity.

If you have a Creative Cloud subscription, Lightroom 4 is now included. If you don't, you'll need to buy it separately, but in the face of competition from the likes of Apple Aperture, Adobe cut the price of Lightroom significantly on its latest release.

Chapter 2
Photoshop tools

Photoshop's engineers add new tools to their
venerable image editing suite with every release. No
wonder it's stayed at the top of its game for so long.

•

Although the choice of available tools may at first
seem too wide to take in they've actually been
broken down into logical groups, with related tools
gathered together in fly-out menus on the tools
panel, so when you know how one works you'll
understand its siblings, too.

•

In this chapter we'll walk you through the most
commonly-used tools, show you where to find
them, which shortcuts you can use to save
yourself time, and how you can use their built-
in parameters to change the way they work.

How to use the built-in brushes
– and how to create your own

Before we begin, we need to explain the difference between the pencil, brush and pen tools.

The pencil tool can have several different tips; it's no longer restricted to a 1x1 pixel block that you drag across the canvas. It shares many common features with the brush tool, but where the brush tool can create soft-edged lines, you can only produce hard edges with the pencil tool.

The pen tool, on the other hand, is used for creating vector paths based on Bezier curves, and with handles that you can drag to reposition the line or change the tightness and angle of the associated curve.

In this section we will be concentrating on using the brush tool and its various options, but once you have got to know how it works you will be able to transfer a lot of what you have learned to tweaking the pencil tool.

You can call up the brush and pencil tools by pressing 'B' several times to cycle through the various tools.

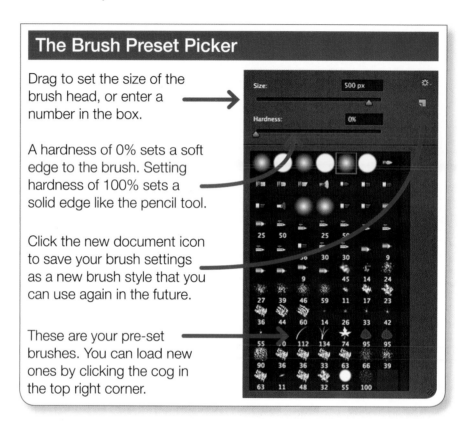

The Brush Preset Picker

Drag to set the size of the brush head, or enter a number in the box.

A hardness of 0% sets a soft edge to the brush. Setting hardness of 100% sets a solid edge like the pencil tool.

Click the new document icon to save your brush settings as a new brush style that you can use again in the future.

These are your pre-set brushes. You can load new ones by clicking the cog in the top right corner.

Choosing a brush

With the brush tool active, click the brush preset picker on the toolbar at the top of the screen. It's the second button along, with a preview of the current brush style used as its icon.

You can see the brush preset picker above. It's split into two sections, with the larger part at the bottom given over to the built-in brush styles. This is where you should start, by clicking the brush shape you need to use. If you can't find one you're after, you can buy or download further brush sets, which are loaded by clicking the cog icon at the top of the picker.

Once you have chosen your basic brush shape, move up to the size and hardness sliders to tweak it to your requirements. The size slider speaks for itself; the hardness slider controls the sharpness of the edges.

Painting with a brush

Now that you've picked your brush you're ready to start using it. In general you can draw on new and pre-existing layers, but you can't mix pixel- and vector-based content, so you can't paint on the same layer as a vector shape or text.

Clicking and dragging with your mouse or using a graphics tablet and pen will draw shapes that match the path of your pointer about the canvas.

However, holding shift while dragging confines the movements to only vertical or horizontal strokes, allowing you to draw straight lines with ease. If you need to create straight lines in any other direction, such as diagonals, hold shift while clicking at the start of the line, then let go of the mouse button, move your mouse to the new position, and click again, with shift still held down. Photoshop will draw a straight line between the two points.

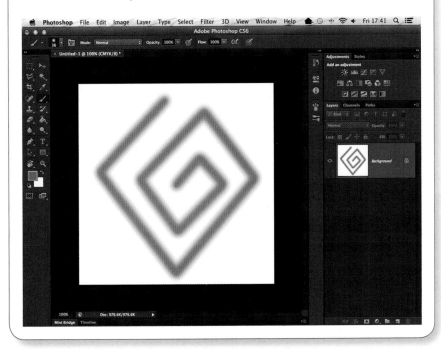

Flow, opacity and tablets

Photoshop works just as well with a graphics tablet and pen as it does with a mouse. This is particularly the case when using brushes, as you can set it to react to the pressure you're putting on the tablet by increasing or decreasing the opacity of the laid down stroke or the size of the brush. Either of these options can be activated using the toolbar at the top of the screen with the brush tool selected.

Even if you don't have a tablet you can still make changes to the strength of the brush using the opacity and flow drop-downs on the same toolbar.

Flow effectively controls the weight of the digital paint laid down on the canvas, while opacity is used to specify how much of the underlying layer it allows to show through. The result in either case is only subtly different.

How to use brushes to create a light particle blog header background

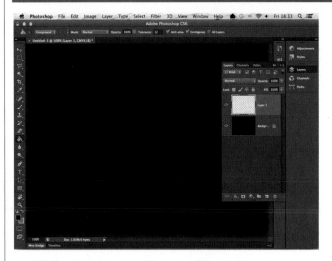

01 Fill the background layer with a dark colour to sit behind your twinkling lights or stars. We have chosen black, but you don't need to do the same if your blog uses a different colour scheme. Create a new empty layer above this to contain your stars.

02 Select the brush tool (shortcut B) and click on the drop-down menu to open the Brush Preset picker. Choose a round brush and set the size fairly small, and the hardness to 100% so that you maintain crisp edges on each of the twinkling lights in your image.

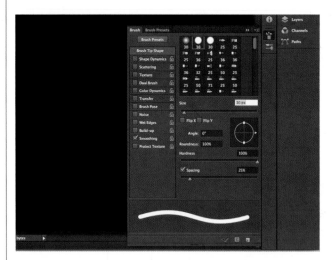

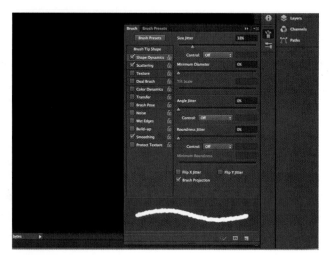

03 Now open the Brush panel by clicking the tabbed button beside the Brush Preset picker on the toolbar. This panel lets you make fairly radical changes to the style of your brush and how it reacts as you stroke it across the canvas. We'll set it up to produce fairly random results.

04 Click Shape Dynamics in the sidebar and drag the Size Jitter slider to the right. By default your brush tip will always stay the same diameter as you drag it across the canvas, but we want it to change slightly as it lays down the lights on our canvas, hence the jitter.

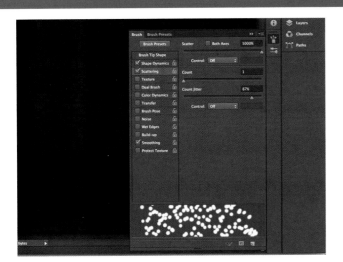

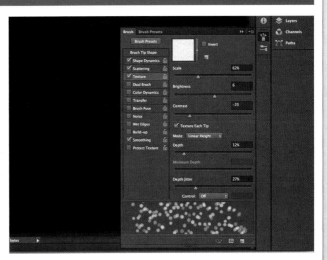

05 Now click on Scattering. To produce a realistic result we need the brush to scatter separate particles of light around the canvas, so drag the scatter slider right to the far end of the scale to make it entirely random, and the drag the Count Jitter in that direction, too.

06 Switch to texture and pick a series of random settings, paying particular attention to brightness and contrast. Keep an eye on the preview at the bottom of the panel. As you can see, our light spots are starting to shine through each other, which is exactly what we want.

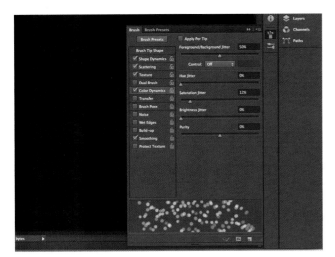

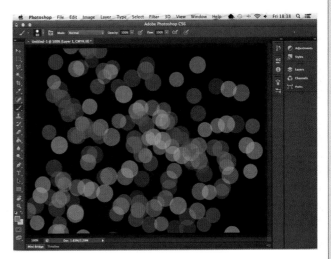

07 Finally, check that the foreground and background jitter is set to 50% and that there is a small value in the Saturation Jitter box. These two effects will make it look like your lights are closer to and further away from your viewer for a more realistic result.

08 Click on the canvas to close the Brush palette and start painting on the new layer. You'll see that rather than forming a continuous line your brush now scatters seemingly random dots of light around itself, which look like defocussed lights or stars in the sky.

Move tool (shortcut: V)

As its name and icon each suggest, the move tool is used for shifting objects around your canvas. It has a few associated options and can automatically switch you to the transform tool if required.

Direct selections

Clicking on the canvas selects the uppermost object in that position. Dragging will then move it around the canvas.

If you find that you have selected something other than the object you want to work with, there are several other methods you can use to select other objects on the canvas.

First, you can resort to the Layers panel, which sits in the sidebar to the right of the interface. If it isn't visible, pick Layers from the Window menu or press the F7 key. Each layer is represented by a thumbnail that will help you identify its contents if you can't tell what it is from its name (only text layers are automatically named, using the contents of the text

string itself). It's always a good idea to keep this visible if you can, as in its default state the move tool doesn't indicate what has been selected on the canvas itself, so you could start to move things unintentionally when you believed you had selected something else.

By keeping the Layers panel open you can see which layer you have selected, as it will be highlighted. Further, you can directly select a layer of choice by clicking it here before going on to manipulate it in the canvas window. Note that

the name of the selected layer also appears in the current document tab of title bar.

Second, you can right-click (on a Mac with a one-button mouse, hold down control while clicking) and select the layer you want from the menu that pops up (see above). Again, it helps if you have named your layers logically so you know what to select here.

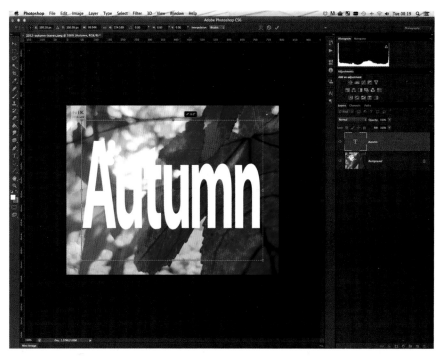

Third, and perhaps most conveniently, you can hold down the command key on the Mac or the ctrl key on Windows to automatically select the uppermost element in the layer stack at the point where you click the canvas.

Automatic selections

You can also task Photoshop with making a sensible guess on your behalf by switching to whichever layer holds the content you have clicked. In the example graphic to the left, if the background layer was active, then clicking on the word Autumn with the move tool wouldn't automatically select it unless we held down ctrl or command, as detailed above, to temporarily enable auto select.

However, by checking the box beside Auto Select (see below) we could enable it permanently. This means that because Autumn was

» *Selecting the option to enable the transform controls adds grab handles to the edges and corners of your on-canvas elements.*

uppermost in the stack it would be automatically selected when we clicked on it, even if the Background was the active layer at that point.

Repositioning the move tool away from the word Autumn and clicking again would select whatever was at the top of the stack at that point – in this case, the background copy, thus saving us from selecting it in a manual manner.

Move and transform

The Move tool is intimately related to the Photoshop transform function, which lets you drag on-screen elements into different shapes. You can enable transform using the shortcut T, but you can also invoke it directly from Move.

Check the box beside Show Transform Controls on the toolbar (see left) and you'll notice that anything you select in your document adopts grab handles on its corners and edges. Dragging these to any new position immediately switches you to the transform tool to undertake the operation (see above).

When using transform, you can drag to irregular shapes by holding command (Mac) or

Move shortcuts

Although it's called Move, this tool is perhaps better thought of as a select tool for picking layers before repositioning them. Don't confuse its shortcut (V - think of moVe) with the more logical keyboard shortcut M, which actually selects the marquee tool.

ctrl (Windows) while dragging one of the corner handles. This allows you to skew text easily.

Notice that as soon as you start using any of the transform controls the toolbar at the top of the screen changes, allowing you to type in numeric settings for dimensions, locations within the canvas, degrees of rotation and so on.

To the right of the toolbar you'll also see the warp button.

Move tool selection

You can quickly select the Move tool from many of the other Photoshop tools by holding down command (Mac) or ctrl (Windows) to call up the tool's icon, and then use it to manipulate another object.

Warp mode

Warp mode allows you to transform selected objects into radical preset shapes. It's particularly effective when used with text in the same way as is possible in some word

processors, such as the word art feature in Microsoft Word. To the right we'll used it to warp the word Autumn.

Copying objects and constraining movement

The Move tool has a couple of hidden features. Hold alt before clicking and dragging on an object and you'll create a new copy, which moves around the canvas independently of the original. Hold shift while dragging and you'll constrain the movements of your objects to exactly horizontal or vertical, or 45% in any direction from the corner of the original element.

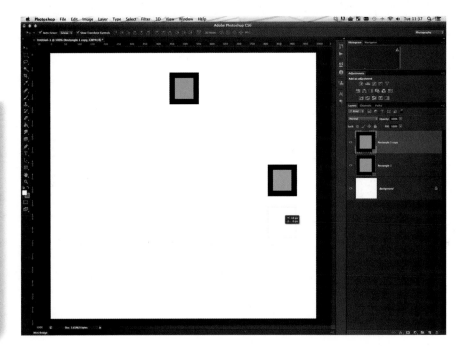

How to use the Warp tool

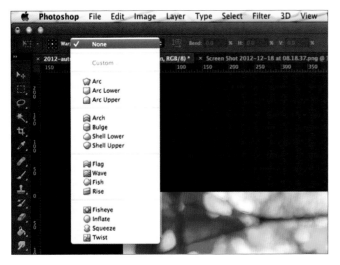

01 Once you've entered the warp tool you first need to select the rough shape you'd like to use. You can then go on to refine it so don't worry if you don't see exactly what you're after. We're going to use the Rise shape.

02 Immediately this had made a big difference to our word but we want to take things further so it looks like it's blowing with the leaves. We'll start by dragging the grab point in the top left of the word to reposition it.

03 Now we're using the input boxes on the toolbar at the top of the screen to exaggerate the sweep and the size differences between the start and end. Experiment here, and don't forget to also try negative numbers.

04 Now that we've finished we click the tick on the toolbar to confirm it and we're returned to the canvas. Despite having made some pretty dramatic changes, the text remains editable, so we can change it at will – here, to Summer.

Marquee tool (shortcut: M)

The **Marquee tool** comes in four different flavours, as you can see from the menu to the right, which appears when you hold down the mouse button on its icon in the toolbox. Tapping M several times cycles between the rectangular and elliptical marquee tools (see right).

The marquee is used for selecting the contents of an

area, rather than a complete layer (for which you use the Move tool). In this respect it is often the best tool to use when you want to copy a block of your image from one part of the canvas to another without using the clone stamp too.

You can constrain the size and shape of the selected area using the options on the top toolbar (see below left) or hold down the shift key while dragging out the selection with the mouse to select a perfect square when using the rectangular marquee tool, or a perfect circle when using the elliptical marquee tool. These modifier keys can also be used with several other tools,

Defining your selection with the Marquee tool

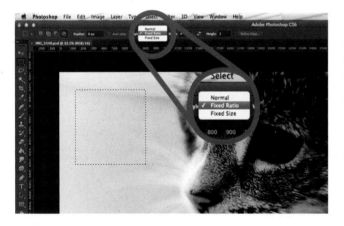

Any of the Marquee tools can be set to maintain specific proportions. Select from the drop-down menu in the middle of the toolbar and use the boxes to its right either to enter specific pixel dimensions or ratios, such as 1:1, 4:3 or 3:2 depending on your requirements.

The four buttons on the left of the top toolbar control how your selections interact with other selections. The second button, Add to Selection, will cause any newly-selected area to be selected without deselecting the existing area so that all of them are manipulated in sync.

Feathering

Feathering lets you soften the transition between the selected and deselected areas in your image. It's controlled using the Feather box on the toolbar and, should you fill a feathered selected area you'll notice that the fill fades out towards the edges and corners. Likewise, if you delete the selected area is will fade out towards the centre of the selection. Note that feathering also causes a rounding off of the corners, as you can see below.

including the vector tools that we'll come to later, where they will similarly constrain their proportions.

The single row and single column marquee tools each make a one-pixel selection stretching across the full width or height of the canvas respectively and are often useful for clearing the edges of an image or building up repeating patterns.

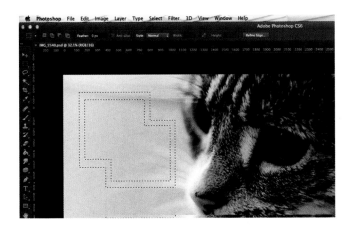

The third button in subtract from selection. With any area already selected, clicking this button and then marking out a new area will cause any parts of that new selection that overlap the existing selection to be deselected. Here, we have deselected the central portion of our shape.

The fourth button is intersect, which allows you to mark out an area on the canvas, and then draw out one or more subsequent areas. Each time you draw a new area, the only parts of that and the original selection that will be kept are those that overlap each other.

Lasso tool (shortcut: L)

Oftentimes you won't want to make such a regular selection as you can with the marquee tool. At times like that you have two options open to you: use the various tools for combining and subtracting areas within the selection, or switch to lasso.

Again, this tool has three different states, which you can cycle through by pressing the L key several times, or holding down the mouse on the button in the toolbox and selecting one of the options from the fly-out menu (see below).

At its most basic – when using the default Lasso setting at the top of the menu – this tool lets you drag a freeform path around your image. When you complete the loop the area inside of it will be selected.

However, this won't always be the most appropriate tool for

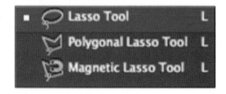

Improving your selection

Sometimes it can be difficult to make an exact selection, as you can see from the magnetic lasso example on the opposite page. At times like this, click the Refine Edge button on the top toolbar to open this panel, which lets you feather the edge of the selection, smooth it off to get rid of any jerky selections and adjust the effect of edge detection, which would hopefully sort out that inaccurately selected ear on the opposite page.

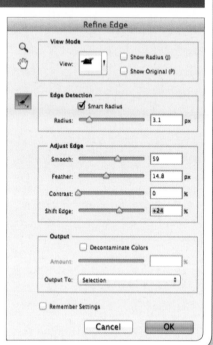

the job at hand, and as you'll see from the opposite page the other two lasso options have very specific actions, which may help you to define the selected area.

A helping hand...

If you are having trouble using something like the magnetic lasso tool, which works best when it has a series of clean, sharp contrasts to follow, open

the channels panel (select it from the Window menu) and isolate the various colour channels in your image in turn to see if one of them provides harsher contrasts. If it does, leave the channels on this setting and perform the magnetic lasso selection. Once you have finished making your selection, re-enable each of the channels by clicking the RGB or CMYK line at the top of the panel.

Lasso tool

The regular lasso tool lets you drag around the area you want to select while keeping the mouse button held down. You'll need to be fairly accurate as they're no assistance. Letting go of the mouse button completes the path and everything that sits inside it will be selected. You can do on to modify the selection using the regular add, subtract and intersect options on the top toolbar and drawing a new selection path.

Polygonal Lasso tool

As its name suggests, the polygonal lasso tool only lets you select in straight lines. It's less suited to organic shapes and more to regular geometry, such as buildings. However, we have used it to select the cat's eye, left, with relative success. You don't need to keep the mouse button held down while defining the path – simply move to the next point each time and click again. Click again on your first point to complete the operation.

Magnetic Lasso tool

The magnetic lasso tool detects hard edges in your image and draws a selection line alongside them as you drag the mouse around. You don't need to keep the button held down, but should return to the starting point and click there when you want to close off the selection. It relies on having a well defined edge to follow. As you can see in the example to the left, it has done a fair job of one ear, but fudged the corners of the other.

Magic Wand and Quick Selection tools

You might question why Adobe has clustered together what appears at first to be two very different tools. Get to know them, though, and you'll see that it was actually a very logical move.

Magic Wand

With the Magic Wand selected, you can click on a colour in your image and have all of the other pixels of a similar colour – within a set tolerance – selected at the same time. It's an easy way to eliminate a particular colour from your image, such as the pink or turquoise fringing you sometimes see on sharp contrasts in photos, and to swap out one particular colour for another.

The tolerance is controlled using an option on the toolbar that runs across the top of the screen, and you can see the effect that various settings have in the box to the right.

The other option you'll find on the toolbar is the contiguous checkbox. When ticked, it will

Working with the Magic Wand

Like all Photoshop tools, the Magic Wand offers a range of options that help you refine the way it works. In the image, above left, we have set too low a tolerance (2) and it has selected only a small portion of the background, as you can see from the outlined area in the upper left-hand corner. We'd now have to click around other parts of the background with shift held down to add them the selection. In the image to the right we have opted for a more appropriate tolerance (32) which has selected more of the background so we will need to spend less time clicking other parts of the image to mop up the rest of the scene. In the image below, we have left the tolerance set to 32, but because

 we clicked a different part of the image as the sample point for our selection which has a similar luminance to the deer (the grass rather than the background), parts of the deer have been selected, too, which we don't want. We'll therefore need to dial down the tolerance.

only select similar coloured pixels that are touching either the place you originally clicked or a pixel that has itself become clicked because it is contiguous with something else closer to the selection point that itself has become selected.

When you first use Photoshop, the Magic Wand will be set to only sample a single pixel when deciding what to select, but you can change this to be a square of pixels between 3 x 3 and 101 x 101 from the sample size drop-down selector on the toolbar.

Rather than using the pure colour of the single point directly under the tip of your wand it instead samples an average of the tones within the selected area and uses these as the reference against which it will compare a similarly average of tones across your image. In images with a fine texture, such as grass on a lawn, fur on a pet or leaves on a tree, this makes it much easier to select a variegated area that would otherwise be fragmented.

Quick Selection

The Quick Selection tool performs a similar function to the Magic Wand, but in a very different manner.

Instead of expecting you to click on the area you want to select, and shift-click to add further patches that were left out of the original selection, the Quick Selection tool lets you paint over the selection instead, while keeping the mouse button held down.

Again, it selects contiguous areas of similar colour, but working this way is often more fluid than using the Magic Wand since you can just keep on painting.

Be careful not to sweep too far without care, as undoing will remove your whole selection.

Crop tool (shortcut: C)

Adobe made a significant change to the crop tool when it released Photoshop CS6: it reversed it.

In previous releases the image being worked on always remained static while you dragged the edges of the crop frame in to the centre of the canvas. In CS6 you still drag the corners and edges of the frame, but at the same time the image repositions itself in the opposite direction so that you only effectively move the pointed half the distance around the screen at any time.

This is the default action in Lightroom, from which Photoshop's new Crop tool was taken, and it allows for much quicker cropping as you won't have to reposition your mouse on the mat or your finger on the trackpad when you run out of space (see below).

There's a well known and highly regarded rule in photography: the rule of thirds. This states that any image in which the key elements are aligned with imaginary

» *The redesigned crop tool in Photoshop CS6 works in the opposite direction to CS5.5 and earlier versions, with the image moving in the opposite direction to the mouse, shortening the time it takes to crop.*

» *The crop tool can also be used to rotate an image. Simply place your cursor outside of the canvas, click and drag. Photoshop automatically resizes the crop to remain within the photo as you rotate it.*

✓ Rule of Thirds
Grid
Diagonal
Triangle
Golden Ratio
Golden Spiral

Auto Show Overlay
✓ Always Show Overlay
Never Show Overlay

Cycle Overlay
Cycle Overlay Orientation

» *You can overlay the active area in the crop tool with a range of common photographic composition guides*

divisions one third of the way in from the left and right edges, and one third of the way in from the top and bottom edges, is more powerful and appealing. The crop tool makes it easy to recompose your images with these rules in mind by overlaying the crop grid with various guidelines, including the rule of thirds. You can select the appropriate grid from the top toolbar.

Once again, the crop tool is multi-modal, and pressing C cycles through the various options, the second of which

is the Perspective Crop tool, which allows you to trim out irregularly shaped objects.

Perspective Crop

The default crop tool, as described above, can only trim down your image using regular straight lines. It's great for recomposing a regular scene, but not so useful when it comes to cropping out parts of an image shot at an angle.

For that you need to switch to the perspective crop tool, which saves you having to

How to: Make irregular crops with the Perspective Crop tool

01 Here we have zoomed in on a canvas that appears in our picture. It was shot while hanging on a wall, from slightly off to one side. Having selected the perspective crop tool, we first click on each corner in turn, working on a clockwise or anti-clockwise direction. In the example below left we have started in the top left corner, and clicked in the two bottom corners. We're now moving up to the upper right corner to click one final time. As you can see, this action is overlaying the image with a perspective grid.

02 With all four corners marked out, Photoshop knows which part of the image we want to retain and – theoretically – where the straight edges actually lie. We now just need to click the tick icon on the toolbar running across the top of the screen and it will crop out the selected area and perform a scale and skew operation on it so that it is reconstructed as a regular rectangular photo, as you can see above. Of course, you don't only have to work with hanging photos – you can skew anything, including a whole wall.

mark it out manually using the polygon marquee tool and then skew the result using the transform tool, all in one action, saving you from working out how to reshape it yourself.

Slice tool

The slice tool, and its ally, the slide selection tool, are slight anomalies here since they don't so much deal with cropping out unwanted portions of an image, and are instead used to slice an image into different sections. Each of these sections can be recomposed on a web page, with different compression

How to: Use the Slice and Slice Selection tools

We have drawn out several slices on the image above. The arc of trees behind the waterfall need to be compressed lightly to retain the foliage detail, so they sit in three slices of their own. The text, too, needs light compression, and will be turned into a link, so it has a slice of its own. The dark water and the waterfall itself can be more highly compressed since they are less detailed, so again they have been set out into separate slices. We're ready to start manipulating them.

To do this we switch to the Slice Selection tool and click first on the Welcome to Scotland line, followed by the properties icon on the toolbar at the top of the screen. This lets us set a destination to which visitors will be sent if they click it, and the appropriate matching alt text. We only want to do that for this single slice, so

when done we can close the properties inspector, and click File | Save for Web to export it.

As can be seen in the grab below, we can now click on each slice in turn and use the compression settings in the sidebar to change the level for each one.

Once we have finished setting the individual compression levels we click the Save button and export the individual slides and the required HTML that stitches them together to a folder on our hard drive, ready to FTP to our site.

levels applied to each part. Why? Because by selectively compressing some parts more – the less important or flatter parts, for example, you can reduce the amount of time it

takes your page to load in the browser and reduce the amount of bandwidth consumed, possibly reducing hosting costs.

You can also use it to create an image map, whereby

clicking different parts of the sliced image in the browser will take your visitor through to different parts of your site. We'll show you how to do that in the boxed out text above.

Healing tools (shortcut: J)

The various healing tools are among the most radical you'll find anywhere in the Photoshop interface, being at once extremely powerful and very easy to use.

They automate a lot of the hard work you would otherwise have to do to remove unwanted objects in your images, with very impressive results. Better yet, with every release of Photoshop, their efficiency seems to improve.

Press the J button to rotate through each of the tool's various functions.

Red Eye tool

If you frequently take pictures of friends and family with the flash – perhaps in a dimly-lit pub or home, or because you're trying to compensate for the sun being right behind them – you'll know exactly what we mean when we talk about red eye. It's an unwanted effect that occurs when the flash bounces off the back of the eyeball and shines straight back into the

camera lens, illuminating the blood in the eye and giving your subjects a pair of red eyes.

The red eye tool is a one-click fix that lets you click in the centre of each red eye and have Photoshop cover it up for you. It detects the edges of the red area and applies a covering fill with an opacity of your choice. It's very fast and effective.

Spot healing brush

We're going to be working on the image above, which doesn't have any red eyes in it, but

is slightly spoiled by the two people standing in front of the castle tower to the right of the frame. We'll use the various healing tools, starting with the spot healing brush, to remove them so that it looks like we had the place to ourselves.

This brush doesn't take any colours or allow you to change its opacity, as all you're doing with it is directing Photoshop's attention to the part of the image that you want to edit. On the opposite page, we've used it to paint over the man who has his back to us. We have slightly

» *The spot healing brush lets you paint over an unwanted object (or person) in your photo and have them automatically swapped out for a pattern built up by sampling its surroundings.*

overlapped the edges and included some of the brickwork of the tower. Photoshop indicates the selected area by colouring it black.

As soon as we let go of the mouse it gets to work and, by examining the surrounding area, it is able to remove the man and fill in the space that he once occupied with a pattern that blends effectively with his surroundings – in this case the ancient brick work.

As you can see from the image above right, the result is pretty impressive, and all we need to do now is sort out the two small green smudges where his feet once stood, which have sucked up some of the grass that surrounded them.

Sometimes, though, the spot healing brush might have a little bit more trouble, which is when you'd resort instead to the healing patch tool, to sample from elsewhere.

Healing patch tool

The healing patch tool works a little like the clone stamp in that it requires first that you define which part of the image you want to sample when repairing another part.

This would let you fix any rare problem repairs that aren't convincing when using the spot healing brush tool, or to sample a different part of the image if you want to replicate a patter

from there in another spot, while blending the transition between the two area in the new location.

Once you have selected the tool, hold alt while clicking the area you want to use as the reference point for the sample that will be reproduced in place of the object you want to replace. Now let go of alt and start painting over the object to be removed and you'll see that the sampled area is copied across. We're in the process of doing just this in the image above right, and have so far

» *The healing patch tool lets you sample content from within your image and use it in place of an object you want to remove.*

removed all but the lady's legs and feet by sampling an area higher up the tower brickwork.

Patch tool

The patch tool works two ways. You start by defining an area within your image by dragging out a freeform lasso selection (see the lasso section for more information) using the patch tool itself and then select on the options bar at the top of the screen whether you want to use that as the source of your patching operation or the destination. Select source if you want to copy your selection to another part of your image, and destination if you want to use another part of your image to replace the selection.

How to: Use the Content-Aware Move tool

Rather than removing people from our image, we'll use the heal tools to rearrange them.

The two people in the castle photo aren't standing very close together. By repositioning them so that they are not so far apart we can make it look like they are having a nice day out. To do this we'll use the Content-Aware Move tool and shift each of them in opposite directions. The original photo is shown above on the left. The edited version is shown above on the right.

We started work on the man. As you can see in the first image, we have used the Content-Aware Move tool to draw a loose selection around him. We've included some of the wall beyond him and the grass on which he's standing as we want to make absolutely certain that he is repositioned with a nice clear edge.

Once we have completed the selection loop we simply drag him to his new position, to the right, and allow Photoshop to generate the missing part of the wall where he was originally standing, and also smooth the edges around his new position.

With him in his new spot we need to do the same to the person on the right. You might imagine this would be tricky as she's wearing a black coat and standing in front of a darker part of the castle. However, we only need to use the same principle, and leave some slack around the figure so that some of the surroundings are also copied across.

We now drag them to the left and Photoshop fixes the sharp contrast between the previous dark background and the lighter castle wall that runs down the left hand side of the new location.

Now simply drag the selected area across your canvas either to the object you want to replace with it (if you had selected 'source') or to the element with which you want to replace the selection (if you had selected 'destination') and Photoshop will apply the relevant edit and smooth the edges. We have used the Patch tool to increase the number of windows in the tower from two to four in the image on the far left.

Clone stamp and pattern stamp tools (shortcut: S)

The clone stamp tool preceded the healing tools we explored in the previous section by several years.

It works in a similar way to the healing patch tool, requiring first that you select source material that is then copied to another part of your image. It doesn't make any effort to smooth the join between the original content and the cloned material that you paint over it.

You can select different brush types from the options bar at the top of the screen, though, and adjust the softness of their edges, which will help to blend the source with its destination surroundings.

The clone stamp tool lets you use the same blending modes as you can for regular layers (see the layers section towards the back of this book) so you can use the source material to

Stamp tool uses

Although we have used the clone and pattern stamp tools to reproduce existing objects in new locations, they are often most useful when correcting imperfections in your image.

DSLR users will know that the sensors in those cameras can sometimes attract dust that shows up as dark spots on the image. These are most often obvious in areas of flat colour such as the sky of grass.

In these instances you could use the spot healing brush to blend them away, but if you want to take more control of what is used to replace them then the clone stamp tool will allow you to select a specific existing element from elsewhere in your image and copy it over the top of the unwanted spot.

You can use the same technique to remove spots, moles and blemishes from peoples' faces in your portraits.

How to use the clone stamp

01 Here's a photo of an isolated house in Scotland, just outside of Glencoe. Part of its beauty is the fact that it has no neighbours, but let's imagine that we want to put forward a proposal to build a small holiday complex in the area using similar houses. The easiest way to illustrate the effect it would have on the surroundings would be to use the clone stamp tool to replicate the building.

change the appearance of the destination without explicitly replacing the original contents with the copied material. Likewise, you can adjust the opacity of the cloned material in its new location, which is particularly useful if using, say, a darken or lighten blend mode as it means you can adjust the strength of the effect.

Note the Aligned Sample check box to the right of the options bar. When ticked, this will always move the source reference point in relation to the current cursor position, even when you're not painting a copy onto the canvas. Unchecking it means that the reference point will always revert to your original position as soon as you release the mouse button, so it's a useful option to disable if you will need to reproduce a single item several times.

02 Start by selecting the Clone Stamp tool and then use the options bar at the top of the screen to choose a medium size brush with a soft edge so that your cloning isn't immediately obvious at the point where the hard edges press up against the existing surroundings. Hold down alt while clicking on the centre of the reference house and then move the mouse to the intended destination.

03 Hold down the mouse button and paint a copy of the source material in its new location. As you can see in the previous image, we were half way through copying the first house. The source reference point will move in sync with the brush painting the copy so that the further you move from the starting point, the more of the original material you will reproduce.

How to use the pattern stamp tool

01 The pattern stamp tool doesn't clone an area you have recently selected, but instead reproduces patterns that you have previously saved. You can use anything as a pattern, so sticking with out Scottish landscape we have selected the house in the photo by using the rectangular marquee to define our chosen area and then selected Edit | Define Pattern... Each pattern needs to be given a unique name, so we have chosen to call this one House so that we can easily find it in the future.

02 Next we switch to the pattern stamp tool, either by holding down on the stamp tool icon until the sub-menu pops out and picking it from there, or by pressing the shortcut key S until it cycles around to the pattern stamp tool. We now need to tell Photoshop which pattern we want to use. The new House pattern is saved in our pattern library, which we can access from the options bar at the top of the screen. As it's the most recently saved one, it's easy to find as it appears at the end of the list.

03 Now all we need to do is paint in the pattern in exactly the same way as we did with the regular clone stamp tool. With the option bar's aligned box ticked it won't matter where you start painting as your patterns will always be aligned to an invisible underlying grid. Unchecking it lets you position your pattern – the house, in this case – wherever you want on the canvas. Enabling the impressionist option treats your pattern like regular wet paint, so passing over the same spot several times smears the result.

Eraser tools (shortcut: E)

Photoshop has three eraser tools to choose from, each of which performs a subtly different function. You can cycle between them by pressing E several times until you arrive at the one you want to use.

Although they remove rather than create content, they are brush-based tools, so you can pick the usual brush types from the options bar at the top of the screen, and change their shapes, opacity and hardness. You can also use the flow control to change the rate at which the erasing effect is applied.

The standard eraser tool removes the convent of your canvas in the usual manner, either filling the space with your selected background colour or punching a hole through to the transparent background (see below).

The background eraser and magic eraser, which we cover over the page, simplify the task of removing areas from more complex images without losing fine detail.

How to use the standard eraser tool

 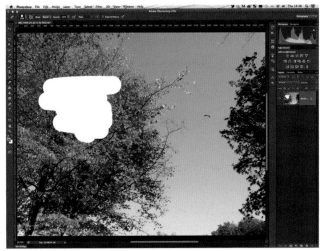

» *The behaviour of the default eraser tool depends on the status of the layer you're working with. In the image above left we are erasing part of a layer that sits above the background (the background is hidden), so the contents are removed and we can see through to the transparent checked board below. In the image on the right we are performing the erase on the background layer itself. As this hasn't been unlocked we are unable to punch a hole in it to reveal the transparency, and so the eraser instead paints over the image using the selected background colour – in this case, white.*

Background eraser

The background eraser works by detecting differences between the centre of the eraser tool and its surroundings.

Select it from the eraser sub-menu and the pointer changes to a circle with a crosshair in the centre. Change the size of the brush as appropriate using the options bar at the top of the screen. Use a larger brush for bigger, flat areas, and a smaller brush for more detailed erasing.

Now start erasing the parts of the image you don't want, being careful to keep the crosshair on the background colour you want to remove. If you do, any other pixels of that colour that fall within the scope of the brush head will also be removed at the same time, without affecting pixels of any other colour that you pass over.

Be careful when approaching areas of fine detail, keeping the crosshair in the centre of the brush outline on a colour that you want to remove. As can be seen in the image above left, we are using the background eraser to remove the flat blue sky, and by keeping the crosshair off the leaves themselves Photoshop is able to remove all of the blue that also appears between the leaves and branches so that they can stray across an otherwise transparent background.

Magic eraser

The magic eraser works in a similar manner, but rather than relying on you painting across the parts of the image you want to remove it allows you to simply click once on the selected colour and it's erased automatically (above right).

Use the Contiguous check box on the options bar at the top of the screen to select whether the pixels that are removed have to be touching the area you have erased. Unchecking it will remove all of the pixels of the colour on which you click, even if they are clearly separated from the area in which you're working.

Paint Bucket and Gradient fill tools (shortcut: G)

The Paint Bucket literally floods your canvas with colour. If you're using it on an empty layer it will cover the whole canvas. If you're using it on a layer that already contains some pixels, it will flood the selected area until it hits the pixels, and then stop.

By default it floods the area with the current foreground colour, but you can switch to using a selected pattern, as we did with the pattern stamp tool, by picking Pattern from the drop-down menu on the option bar at the top of the screen.

From here you can also set the blending mode and opacity of the fill, and control the tolerance, which specifies how strict it should be at stopping the flood fill when it encounters something else on the canvas.

Gradient fill

Gradient fill works in a similar manner, but rather than using just the foreground colour or a pattern, if uses both the foreground and background colours and transitions between them in its default state, while also offering foreground-to-transparent and a range of preset colour gradients. The chosen gradient style is selected from the drop-down menu on the options bar.

This is also where you pick the style of gradient, using the five buttons to the right of the fill type. You can see the effect of each one in the examples to the right. In each case we have set out foreground colour to red and our background colour to blue and drawn a single straight or diagonal line across the canvas. You can see how radical the differences are between each one.

Gradients are useful for far more than just laying down colour in your image, and are particularly powerful when used to define a layer mask (see the section on layers), with a black-to-white linear gradient controlling the visibility of an effect, such as a darkening of an otherwise burned-out sky in your image in a non-destructive manner.

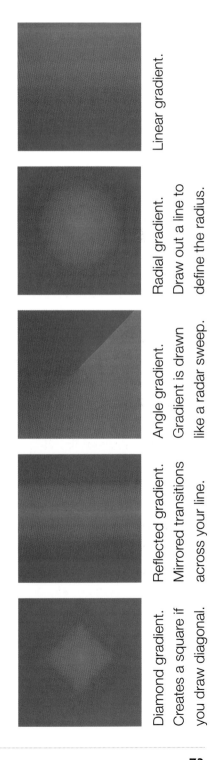

Linear gradient.

Radial gradient. Draw out a line to define the radius.

Angle gradient. Gradient is drawn like a radar sweep.

Reflected gradient. Mirrored transitions across your line.

Diamond gradient. Creates a square if you draw diagonal.

73

Blur, sharpen and smudge tools

Blur, sharpen and smudge are effectively correction tools. Blur lets you apply a soft focus effect to portraits or remove details like number plates from images in which they shouldn't be visible. Sharpen increases the contrast on edges and gives your image a bit more kick. Smudge runs one part of the canvas into the next in line with your mouse movements across the image.

However, while they may most often be used for applying corrections, they can also be used in a creative manner.

Blur

The most obvious creative use for the blur tool is to simulate a shallow depth of field in your images. This is usually achieved by shooting the subject with a camera using a wide aperture lens, but if this isn't possible, or you're working with an existing image with a long depth of field, you'll need to apply the effect in software by carefully tracing around the subject (perhaps having first masked off a selection) so that you don't encroach on the subject matter itself.

The result of blurring the background will be to draw your viewer's eye towards the subject itself and give the whole image a single point of focus.

How to use the smudge tool

» *The smudge tool treats the canvas as though it is covered in wet paint. Holding down the mouse button and dragging around the image smears the contents in the direction in which you're dragging. Adjusting the strength setting on the options bar at the top of the interface changes the effective pressure you're putting on the canvas. Setting it to 100% will preserve the original starting point as it's dragged around. Choosing a lower setting (in the image above right we have chosen 44%; the image above left is the original) lets the original selection slowly slip away and has a lighter effect on the rest of the canvas.*

If you need to blur more than just a selected area, use one of the blur filters from the Filter menu. Gaussian blur is often the most effective.

Sharpen

If you're working with a slight defocussed image, selective use of the sharpen tool can go a long way towards fixing it.

This is particularly true where portraits are concerned.

Applying the sharpen tool to the eyes – particularly the corners and outlines – is often enough to disguise myriad photographic problems, as this is the first part of the picture that viewers look at. If the eyes are sharp, the assumption is that the rest of the image is, too.

Smudge

The smudge tool acts like a thumb on an oil-painted canvas and is particularly useful if you have been working with brushes and want to create a hand-made finish to your work.

Smudging lets you push a colour from one part of the canvas into another, adjacent part where the two will mix as though they are wet. The degree to which they combine, and the distance through which you can spread the colours depends on the strength setting chosen on the options bar.

How to use the blur and sharpen tools

» *The sharpen and blur tools work in opposition to each other. Here we are using the sharpen tool. The original image is shown on the left, zoomed to 100%; the edited version is shown on the right. Again, we have set the strength to around half of its maximum limit. As you can see from the result, the texture of the underlying metal is far more obvious on the edited version. The blur and sharpen tools work with greater force the more you pass over the same point. It therefore pays to set the strength to a lower level than you might expect and perform several repeats.*

Dodge, burn and sponge tools (shortcut: O)

Each of these is a digital reproduction of a traditional photographer's tool, and although you can use them on original artwork that you have created in Photoshop itself, they are more effective when used as correctional measures for your photos.

Each of the tools performs a very specific purpose, and anyone who is familiar with print-based photography and manual paper exposure should find them immediately familiar.

Dodge

When old school photographers found that part of their image was too dark they would use an opaque material – often card – to obstruct the light as it passed from the exposing machine towards the sensitive paper.

With less light reaching the paper it would be exposed for a shorter time, and the result would be that it wouldn't turn so dark.

Photographers working this way would usually shake the card so that there were no hard edges to the obscured area. This action was known as dodging, and it's a term that has been carried across into the digital realm for the equivalent tool.

How to use the dodge tool

01 This picture was taken at night in a dimly lit room. It is fairly well balanced, but the cat's face is too dark. We can use the dodge tool to lighten it up by decreasing the saturation of the colours in the face so that, if we were working in the old analogue world of photo printing, more of the white paper would show through.

02 Having selected the dodge tool we now need to choose an appropriate brush. We will be lightening the whole of the cat's face so we're using the two sliders to create a large brush with a soft edge (by setting a hardness of 0%). We will leave all of the other settings on the options bar in their default positions.

Restricting the affected tones

Most often you'll only want to brighten (dodge) shadows and mid-tones or darken (burn) highlights and mid-tones. You can therefore pick any one of these three options from the options bar at the top of the screen when using the dodge and burn tools so that you don't either lose dark areas in complete shadow, or burn out lighter areas entirely.

Burn

The burn tool does just the opposite to dodge, and again it has its roots in traditional photography, where to darken off overexposed areas, such as skies that had been bleached out, the photographer would allow some parts of the paper to be exposed for longer, effectively burning the image onto the page.

Sponge

Finally, the sponge tool adjusts the saturation of the image. It can be used to boost colours in any part of your picture that is wishy-washy and lacking punch without affecting the whole of the canvas.

The easiest way to think about it is to imagine that you are using a sponge with a pattern cut into it to transfer ink from a saucer onto the paper as you might have done at school.

You can use the sponge tool in reverse, too, by picking desaturate from the option bar.

03 We're now painting over the cat's face. In some places we need to perform two passes over the particularly dark areas to bring them up to a level we are happy with. We are paying particular attention to the eyes, which we want to brighten, and also trying to balance out the darker left side, which was away from the light.

04 Now that we've finished, we can compare what we had at the start of the process with what we have achieved using just the dodge tool. Because we chose a soft-edged brush we haven't had to be too careful about not going over the edges of the face, so the result is smooth and free of obvious joins.

Pen tool (shortcut: P) and paths

The pen tool is a bit of an anomaly in Photoshop. Most of the work you do in the application will involve the manipulation of raster graphics – effectively pixels sitting beside other pixels.

The pen tool, on the other hand, deals with vectors, which are coordinate-based descriptions of points on your canvas, and the lines and curves that join them. These form paths, which are stored in the paths panel.

Getting started with paths

Before we go any further, you'll need to call up the paths panel so that you can see what's going on behind the scenes. Click Window | Paths, and you'll see it appear in the sidebar. Now switch to the pen tool either by selecting it from the toolbox or using the shortcut P.

Pressing that button several times cycles between the regular pen tool and the freeform version, which lets you draw irregular shapes on the canvas.

Each path needs to be a complete, closed-off loop; until you have closed it, each subsequent click with the pen

Drawing your first shape

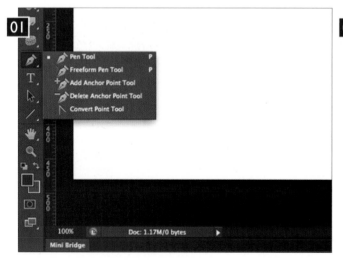

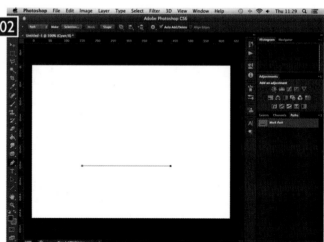

The pen tool can work with both straight lines and curves, automatically selecting between the two depending on whether you click or drag on the canvas.

To demonstrate how each works, we'll draw a semi-circle, which encompasses both.

Start by selecting the Pen tool from the fly-out menu [01] and then click at either end of the line that will form the base of your semi-circle [02]. Holding down shift while clicking the second point will

Quick fact: the curves created by the pen tool are called Bezier curves, and are named after Pierre Bezier, a designer for the French automobile company Renault who, although he didn't invent them, is credited with being the first person to fully appreciate how useful they could be as a design element.

tool will just extend the path until you return to your start point.

The pen tool graphic gives you visual feedback on the status of your path. When you first select the tool, or when you are not working with an active path, you'll notice that there's an asterisk beside its icon as you move it around the canvas.

As soon as you click the first vector of your path, the asterisk disappears to indicate that further clicks will add to the path. When you hover over the starting point again, the pointer is accompanied by a small circle, which signifies that clicking at that point will close off the path.

Understanding curves

As you'll see in the example below, you can create a straight line by clicking individual points, and create a curve by dragging. The turn of the curve is controlled by a pair of handles, with one on each end. The length of these handles determines the height or depth of the curve, while their angle determines the angle at which the curve launches itself from its point of origin, with the curve initially following the handle before veering off.

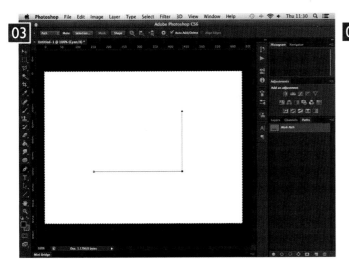

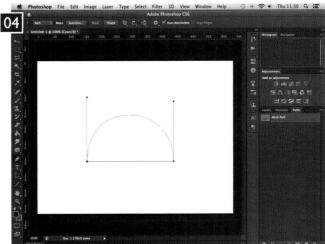

ensure it's lined up with the first one.

Without letting go of the mouse button, drag upwards to create a handle [03] and then let go of both the mouse and the shift key, move back to your first point, and click once more, then drag up the same distance to extend another handle and create the curved top of your semi-circle [04].

When you let go of your mouse this time the path will be completed.

Controlling curves using handles

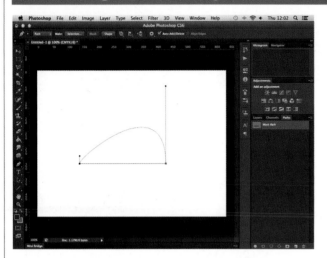

Here, a tall handle to the right produces a higher curve, while a short one to the left gives us a shorter curve. The result is a lopsided curve biased towards the right. Shorter handles at both ends would have given us a shallow curve throughout.

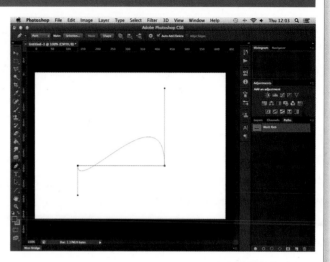

The curve always goes in the same direction as its closest handle, so dragging down on the left of the graphic here draws down the curve so that it sits below the original horizontal line. Dragging down both handles would have made the whole curve sit below it.

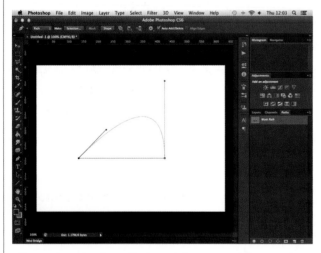

Dragging the handle inwards causes the angle at which the curve leaves its point or original to be sharper. In this case we have dragged it to the right and made the slope shallower on the left, and much sharper on the right where it is pushed against that handle.

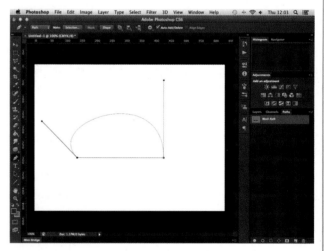

Dragging a handle away from the centre, however, causes the curve to bulge out. The result, as seen above, is a sharper angle on the left of our curve and a shallower take off on the right where it is being pulled away from the first handle in the graphic.

Freeform pen tool

So far we have been using the regular pen tool, but this is accompanied by the freeform, which is accessed from the same fly-out menu as the pen tool, or by pressing the shortcut P for a second time.

This lets you draw an irregular path by hand, rather than using control points and handles. The result will usually be less controlled, lacking straight lines and smooth curves.

Despite this, Photoshop does actually drop a series of control points along the line as you progress, as you'll discover once the path has been completed and you start to work with it, particularly with the path selection and direct selection tools, which we'll cover in the next section.

Manipulating your path

So far we have been drawing our path and assuming that we have got everything right on the first attempt. However,

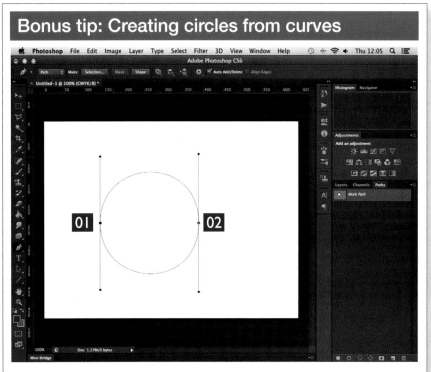

Bonus tip: Creating circles from curves

The pen tool makes it very easy to create a circle with just two strokes. Start at point 01 by clicking on the canvas and dragging down to create a handle. Release the mouse button, then shift-click at point 02 to make sure the two vector locations are aligned and again drag down to create a handle of equivalent length to the first. You'll notice that the bottom half of the circle is immediately created. Finally, release the mouse again and return to point 01, and click to complete the path, and with it your circle.

from time to time you will need to manipulate it after you have plotted its course.

At this point, the add and delete anchor points come in to play. These are also found on the pen tool's fly-out menu, but can't be accessed using the P shortcut, so you'll need to select them in the regular manner using the mouse.

As their names suggest, these add or remove control points on an existing path, such as the ones from which we drew out the handles to control the angle and size of our curves on the examples on the opposite page.

Over the page, we'll show you how to use Add Control Point to create a banner.

How to create a banner using Bezier curves and the pen tool

01 Our starting point is a single word – WINNER – which we've already warped to match the shape of our banner. From here, we use the pen tool to draw a regular rectangle of about the same size.

02 The banner needs to be extruded to that it matches the shape of the word, so we add two new control points – on above and one below – that we can then drag up until the curve top and bottom matches the curve of the text.

03 A path is merely a description of some points in the image. To give it some form in the finished graphic we need to paint along it on a new layer. So, we switch to the Layers panel and create a new layer.

04 Now we switch back to the Paths panel, select the brush tool from the toolbox, our chosen colour (blue) and a weight (10px) then click the second button at the bottom of the Paths panel to apply a blue stroke to the path.

05 Now the tabs. We've created a new layer in the Paths panel, drawn the tab at the end of the banner and used the same stroking method to apply a blue outline, which itself is on a separate layer in the Layers panel.

06 At the moment, the inner edge of the tab is visible within the main part of the banner. We don't want that, so we've selected the inside of the main banner in the Layers panel and used that as a guide to paint white over the tab end.

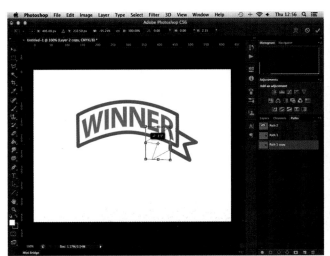

07 We need a tab on both ends, so we've duplicated the first one and used the transform tool (command-T on Mac, ctrl-T on Windows) and dragged the right handle on the bounding box far to the left to mirror it.

08 Now we apply the transformation by switching to the brush tool, repeat the stroking process and once again paint out the part of the tab that shows through the main banner to complete the graphic.

Path Selection and Direct Selection (shortcut: A)

We've already shown you how you can manipulate an existing path by adding new control points and removing points that already exist. Sometimes, though, all you'll want to do is move the ones that already exist. That's when you use the path selection and direct selection tools.

Path selection tool

The path selection tool is the least flexible of the two tools that reside on this particular fly-out menu. With this selected, clicking anywhere on your path will select the whole thing so that when dragged, the complete path moves around the canvas (see below).

Note that even if you have more than one path on a

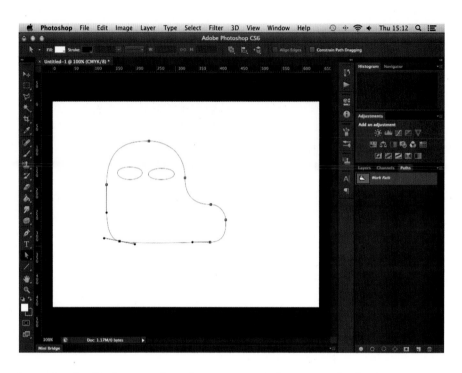

layer in the Paths panel, only the selected layer will move around, and not all of them, unless you drag a selection area around them all using the path selection tool. Dragging them around the canvas will then move them in unison.

Direct selection tool

The direct selection tool, on the other hand, lets you select specific anchor points on the path and move them individually. In the graphic above we have used it to

straighten out the bulging lower left corner of our ghost shape so that it isn't so fat.

As well as moving the control points themselves, we can also reposition their handles to edit the associated curves, as you can see in the more extreme example below.

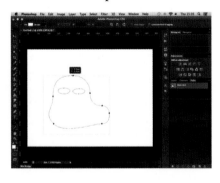

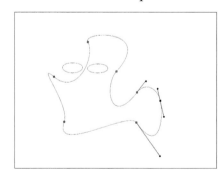

Shape tool (shortcut: U)

The other major vector tool in Photoshop deals with shapes. The six primary shapes – rectangle, rounded rectangle, ellipse, polygon and line – have dedicated spots on the fly-out menu, and you can switch between them with sequential taps of the U shortcut.

You can define the dimensions of the current shape using the options bar at the top of the screen where you can type in dimensions, select the colours for the outline and fill, and the width of the stroke that surrounds it.

A few of the options are shape-specific, such as the setting for the radius of the corners when creating rounded rectangles.

Each shape appears on its own layer in the Layers panel and can be dragged into whichever stacking order you choose. This also allows you to change their opacity and blend modes in the same way you would any other layer (see the section on Layers for more information).

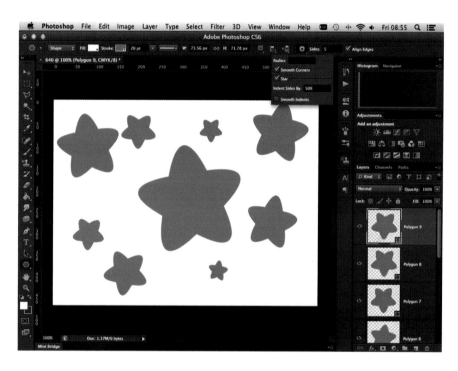

Working with polygons

The polygon tool is the most generic of each option, allowing you to specify the number of sides it should have on the options bar and quickly create stars by using the settings in the further menu that appears when you click on the cog (see above). Enabling smooth corners and smooth indents gives you a child-like rounded star of the kind we have used in the grab above. The radius setting lets you specify an exact size for each one.

Custom shapes

These six core shapes are just a small subset of the options open to you when using the shape tool. You can expand them massively by picking custom shape from the bottom of the tool's fly-out menu and then choosing the shape you want from the options bar. You can further increase the range to include outlines of animals, talk bubbles, frames and so on by picking those sets from the sub-menu (click the cog) or enable them all at once.

T. Type tools (shortcut: T)

There are four basic type tools covering horizontal and vertical type, plus horizontal and vertical type masks.

The latter two make it easy to define which parts of a layer should remain visible so that they form the fill or texture of your type, and reduce what was previously a fairly fiddly job for first-timers to a simple one-click operation. See the panel on the opposite page for how to use them.

Basic type controls

At its most basic, you can add type to the Photoshop canvas in exactly the same way you would in a word processor or DTP application. Simply click on the canvas with the type tool active and Photoshop will give you an insertion point, with the font settings – face, size and so on – reverting to whatever they were the last time you used the tool. If you choose to make any changes, you'll notice that each font name is accompanied by a preview in the drop-down menu so you can see at a glance what it will look like.

Even after typing or pasting your text you can switch between horizontal and vertical type by clicking the button on the far left of the options bar.

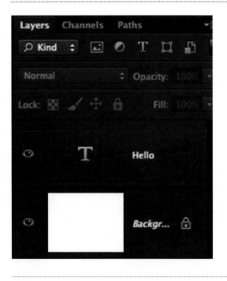

» *Left: Text layers are automatically given a name that reflects their content, such as 'Hello' in this example. If you can't distinguish between several text layers that start with the same characters, expand the layers panel horizontally by dragging its margin into the Photoshop editing area.*

You can enter text in two ways, as either a single text entity or as a paragraph.

To enter a single entity, simply click on the canvas and start typing. Photoshop will continue accepting text for as long as you keep typing and arrange it on a single line that will stretch beyond the boundaries of your canvas if you keep typing. To insert a break in the text you'll need to hit the return key.

This is simple enough, but what happens if you want to edit the text later? There's a chance that this would change the length of each line and your paragraph breaks would end up in the wrong place.

If you want to enter more than one line of text you would therefore do better to define a text area, in much the same way as you would if you were laying out a document using a DTP application such as Adobe InDesign or Quark XPress.

In this instance, rather than simply clicking on the canvas and starting to type, you would click and drag out the text area

Using the type mask tools

The horizontal and vertical type mask tools work in a similar way to the regular type tools, laying down text on your canvas with full control over kerning, leading, font size, angle, and so on.

However, rather than simply placing the text in the usual manner, in which it takes on your chosen colour and sits on the canvas on its own, it is used to define which parts of an associated layer should remain visible. In this way you can use the layer contents as the fill for the text, as you can see in the example below.

Our starting point is a regular image of a castle on a loch, which we have imported into Photoshop, copied from its original document and placed on its own layer in our new file. We have left the background layer in place so that when we apply the mask the characters will be surrounded by white, but you can delete this if you would prefer the characters to sit on a transparent canvas, perhaps because you want to export it for use on the web where it will sit over a graphic background.

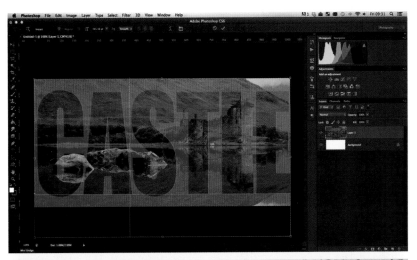

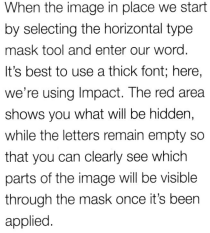

When the image in place we start by selecting the horizontal type mask tool and enter our word. It's best to use a thick font; here, we're using Impact. The red area shows you what will be hidden, while the letters remain empty so that you can clearly see which parts of the image will be visible through the mask once it's been applied.

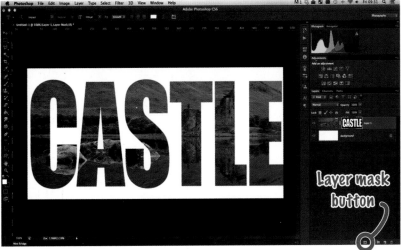

When we're happy with the text, having adjusted the font size and the spacing between the characters for optimal results, we click the mask button at the bottom of the Layers palette twice. The first time it previews the result with a marching ants outline; the second time it applies the mask to hide everything outside of the characters.

Using the character settings panel

The character panel gives you access to all of the options you need to control the appearance of the text in your Photoshop document.

If you have ever used a desktop publishing application then many of its settings will already be familiar, such as font size, leading and kerning.

You can change a setting by picking from a menu (for example, font size), typing into the box and, in many cases, dragging on the setting icon.

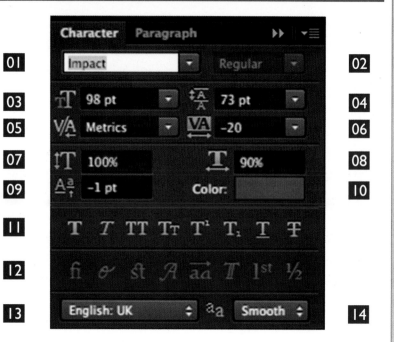

01 | 02 | 03 | 04 | 05 | 06 | 07 | 08 | 09 | 10 | 11 | 12 | 13 | 14

01 Select the font face here. Each font name is accompanied by a short sample of text in that style.
02 Pick the font style, such as light, regular or italic.
03 The font size menu. We're using points as our scale, as this is what we chose in Photoshop's preferences, but you can switch it to pixels if you find that easier to understand.
04 Line spacing setting, again specified in points in our installation.
05 Sets the kerning (space) between two individual characters to help you eliminate unnatural empty space by tightening them up, or separate characters that appear to merge by loosening them.
06 Sets the tracking, which is similar to kerning, but applies to a range of characters, rather than just two side by side and gives the overall text a feeling of looseness or tightness.
07 Set character height as a percentage of the default height for the selected font size.
08 Set character width as a percentage of the default width for the selected font size.
09 Raises or lowers the selected character above or below the regular run of characters.
10 Opens the colour picker to set the character colour.
11 Character style choices such as italic, small caps or underlined.
12 Accesses specific font options such as ligatures, ordinals and stylistic variations. Not relevant to all fonts, so sometimes greyed out, as seen here.
13 Specifies the language in use so that the spell checker can identify typing errors and spelling mistakes, and the correct hyphenation rules can be applied.
14 Chooses the font smoothing option applied to the text (see the panel on the next spread).

container. As soon as you let go, Photoshop would drop your text insertion into the box, ready for you to start typing. As soon as your text reached the right-hand edge of the frame it would automatically soft-wrap down to the next line.

Now, when you make further edits in the future, the text will automatically re-flow, saving you from manually adding and removing paragraph returns as required. You can also resize the text frame with the same result.

Formatting your type

Photoshop has almost as many options for tweaking your text as it does for customising the brushes you use to paint on the canvas. The most obvious options are font face and size, but further examination of the options bar opens up a significant range of varied enhancements.

The vast majority are accessed through the type options panel, which you'll access by clicking the folder icon, above, on the options bar.

The full range of options can initially seem quite bewildering, but by working your way through each section in a logical manner you will quickly come to understand what each element handles.

The full type panel is divided into two sections, organised on separate tabs for characters and paragraphs. You can target anything from a single letter, number or punctuation mark, right up to several highlighted blocks of text using the settings on the character tab. Settings applied through the paragraph tab, though, can only apply to complete paragraphs. As such, if you only want to work with a single paragraph you don't need to select all of its contents, but just click anywhere inside it. Changes you then apply – such as alignment, spacing before the first line and after the last, and so on, will be applied to the complete paragraph automatically. Applying them to more than one paragraph will still require that you select at least some text from each one. This is often achieved most easily either by clicking within the text and using the shortcut command-A (Mac) or ctrl-A (PC) to select all of the text or, if you don't want to format everything, select the last few words of one paragraph and the first few words of the next to style just two sequential paragraphs.

Typographic effects

As well as a first-class text engine, Photoshop can apply a wide range of artistic effects. Text is arranged on layers, so you can use the same blend modes, opacity settings and so on as you would for regular layer content.

However, you can also warp text into a number of creative shapes. As a bonus, doing so doesn't stop you performing further edits to the text in the future.

Start by typing your text in the manner described above and then click the warp button

Font smoothing

Most professionally-designed fonts look great in their default state, but if the result strikes you as either too dull or too sharp, you can adjust it using the anti-aliasing drop-down menu on the options bar. As well as letting you retain the font's default appearance (by selecting None) it gives you the option of four different kinds of anti-aliasing, allowing for sharp, crisp, strong or smooth results, depending on how much you want the text to stand out from its surroundings or complement them. The results will be affected by your choice of font, text size and the characters in question, but as can be seen from the example below, where the O on the left is set to None and the one on the right is set to Smooth, it can make a significant improvement.

on the options bar (see right) to open the warp tool.

As you can see from the grab below, this lets you mould your text into a range of preset shapes, such as an arc, flag, fish and so on. Selecting one will apply it using the default settings, after which you can drag the sliders below the menu to change the individual levels of distortion.

Once you click OK, the warp effect will be applied, but you'll notice that the selected text remains underlined, indicating that it can still be edited, by inserting or deleting characters. As you do, the effect will update in real time.

You can also drag the corners and edges of the text frame to change the size of the rendered characters.

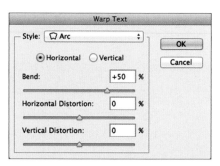

Working with ligatures

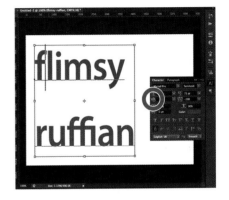

01 The text above is styled using the Myriad Pro font. As you can see, the 'fl' of flimsy and the 'ffi' of ruffian have been joined together to form a single shape in each instance. The result is more attractive that it might otherwise have been, since the top of the 'l' is not crashing into the 'f' and the dot of the 'i' is not lost in the second 'f' of ruffian.

This is because the Standard Ligatures option is enabled in the character panel (circled).

02 Disabling Standard Ligatures removes these adjustments, and now all of the letters are separated by a small space. We can change the space between them by adjusting the kerning. In some peoples' eyes, this will make the 'fl' of 'flimsy' easier to read. However, the benefit of the 'ffi' of 'ruffian' is more difficult to justify. You would therefore do better to disable ligatures on just the first word in this instance, then, and leave 'ruffian' in its default state.

03 An alternative solution would be to leave Standard Ligatures active and insert a space between the 'f' and 'l' of 'flimsy'. Initially this would look unnatural since the gap between the two letters would be too wide, but by selecting the space character we have inserted we can use the kerning control (circled) to draw together the 'f', space and 'l'. As a result, the space effectively disappears while still performing its function.

A word about hyphenation

If you're entering your text as a paragraph rather than a single line, having first drawn out a text frame and then typed into it, be sure to check the paragraph tab and select whether or not you want to enable hyphens.

Excessive hyphenation can be distracting, but lack of hyphenation on narrow columns can lead to unnatural spacing, so use them with care.

Chapter 3
Photoshop layers

Layers are fundamental to unleashing your full potential in Photoshop. Far more than simply an organisational tool for keeping the various parts of your image separate from one another, they're a creative force in their own right.

•

Layers can be stacked in whichever order you choose, grouped into folders, have their opacity tweaked to an almost infinite degree, and be hidden and shown at will. You can use the colour from one layer to tint the texture of another, and use the pattern of an upper layer to mask out unwanted sections on a completely different layer below.

•

It may all sound highly technical, but layers are easy to get your head around with a little bit of practice and, when you do, they'll make a world of difference to your work.

Using Layers to organise your work

Layers first appeared in Photoshop fairly late on – in version 3. It seems almost unbelievable now, with layers being such an important, integral part of the application, that they might ever have been missing.

Adobe itself likens layers to layers of acetate stacked one on top of the other. Acetate is transparent, so the only parts of the acetate that you'd not be able to see through if you were looking down on the acetate stack from above would be the parts on which you have painted. These would therefore block out the same parts of any layer below.

Layers in Photoshop work in exactly the same way. Any part of the layer on which you have painted or laid out an object such as a vector object, photography or string of text, will obscure those same parts of the layers below.

Further – again in a similar manner to physical acetate – if one of the upper layers contains some semi-transparent content, such as a vector with partial transparency, or the feathered edge of a spray-painted area, you will see a lesser or greater portion of the layers below. It is often easier to understand with an example, as seen below.

Understanding the Layers palette

The blending mode menu lets you change the way that the contents of a layer affect those below it. The Opacity guide beside it controls how effectively the selected layer blocks out the content of those that sit below it.

Click the eye icons in the first column to hide each layer.

The uppermost layer contains fully opaque text that blocks out everything below it. The next layer down contains opaque colour at the top, fading to transparency below, so we can boost the sky of the background. The background layer holds our original photo.

The buttons at the bottom of the panel let you add effects, block out specific parts using layer masks, create new layers and group them into folders so that they are easier to manage as your document grows.

A new image, whether it's one you've created from scratch or a photo you've opened from your hard drive or a memory card, consists of just one layer, called Background. You'll notice that this has a padlock beside it, meaning that it has a special status within the document. If you want to make adjustments to it you'll first have to unlock it by double-clicking.

Creating new layers

Some new layers are created automatically. When you type some text or use one of the vector tools, for example, the results are positioned on a new layer. However, at other times you'll want to create layers on the fly. You can do this by clicking the new layer button at the bottom of the layers palette.

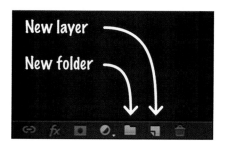

Filtering layers

Photoshop CS6 introduces layer filtering and searching. Use the top line of the layers palette to show or hide specific layer types by content, such as text, adjustments, vector art or bitmaps.

You can delete a layer by selecting it within the palette and clicking the trash icon in the row of buttons at the bottom of the interface.

Organising layers

You'll have noticed from the image below left that beside the new layer button there's also a new folder icon. Clicking this creates an empty folder within the layer stack into which you can drag one or more existing layers, and inside of which you can create new layers.

Doing this helps greatly when it comes to keeping your layers in check.

For example, in a complex editing job your document can quickly grow to become several dozen – or several hundred – different layers. Keeping each of these on view the whole time is impractical as the layers list

The layers palette

If the layers palette isn't currently visible, you'll need to turn it on. Either pick it from the View menu, or press F7 on your keyboard.

will extend below the bottom of the application window and you'll have to keep scrolling up and down to find each one.

Organising them into folders, however, means you can group layers according to their contents or the part of the image to which they relate. So, if you were creating a sci-fi space scene, you might organise everything to do with the surface of the planet into one folder, everything to do with an alien life form you have created into another and so on.

You could then collapse the planet folder when you were working on the alien and vice versa, or turn off visibility of everything in each folder by clicking the eye icon in the margin beside either one, thus giving yourself more room in which to work and allowing you, for example, to work on parts of the planet surface that would otherwise be obscured by the alien in front of it.

You can quickly and easily duplicate existing layers by dragging them from their current position with the layers palette and onto the new layer icon at the bottom of the panel.

Selecting and moving layers within your document

One of the key benefits of working with layers, aside from the fact that it means you can separate out your image components so that editing one part of the picture doesn't mean you undo your good

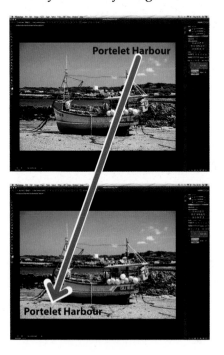

Layer thumbnails

Sometimes it can be difficult seeing what is happening in the layer thumbnails. On these occasions you'll want to enlarge the previews in the layers panel.

Click the lined icon in the top right corner of the palette (you'll find one of these on most palettes, where it's used to access the palette settings) and select Panel Options...

From the dialogue that appears, pick a more appropriate thumbnail size, bearing in mind that with larger thumbnails you'll be able to display fewer at any one time within the palette.

If you're still having trouble working out what's going on from the thumbnail, switch the option below this from showing the complete document area within the thumbnail to just the contents themselves ('Layer Bounds') and Photoshop will dynamically resize the thumbnail contents, making them larger within the box and thus easier to see.

work elsewhere, is that you can reposition elements within the frame just as easily.

There are two ways you can do this, but both require that you have the selection tool active. This appears at the top of the tools palette, and can be invoked by tapping V on the keyboard (see the icon below).

The first, and arguably simplest, is to click on the layer that you want to move in the layers palette and then move to the main document window and drag that layer's contents

» *The Photoshop Move tool (shortcut V).*

to their new position (see the grabs in the left-hand column).

If you haven't been careful to name all of your layers so that they make sense by double-clicking their names in the layers palette and renaming them, you might have to click through several before you find the one you need, so instead of clicking in the palette, so long as the layer is visible, you can hold down command on the Mac, or ctrl on the PC and click directly on the object you want to move within the editing window. Let go of the keyboard buttons and then drag the item in the usual manner.

Master layer masks in four simple steps

The new layer mask appears as a blank canvas attached to the layer. Because it is white it isn't blocking out any of the associated layer. If it was black it would block out everything and we'd see through to the white layer that we have positioned below it.

The layer mask tool looks like a circle on top of an empty canvas. It's found on the toolbar at the bottom of the Layers palette.

01 Every layer can have a mask attached. This blocks out certain parts of the layer and lets other parts show through. We'll use one to create a stylised image of the eyes in this photo. We've opened out original photo, copied the image onto a new layer by dragging it onto the new document icon at the bottom of the Layers palette and then

attached an empty mask by clicking the mask button (circled). Masks work on the basis that more and more of the attached layer is blocked out with the application of ever-darker colours to the mask layer. Always make sure you're painting on the mask and not the original image by clicking the mask thumbnail in the Layers palette.

Ensure you're painting on the mask by clicking here

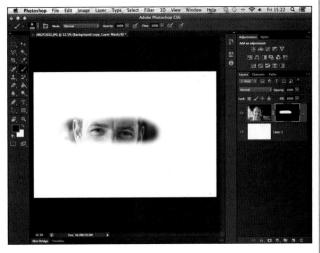

02 So that we can keep track of what we're doing, we'll work in reverse. We've picked a soft-edged brush and set the foreground colour to black, then after clicking on the Layer thumbnail we have started to paint over the areas we want to keep. At the moment it's erasing the eyes and showing instead the white layer below.

03 Now we can invert the mask so that the black areas, which were obscuring the eyes, become white, and the white areas become black, thus blocking out the rest of the layer to show the layer that sits below. Selecting the mask thumbnail and picking Image | Adjustments | Invert, or use the shortcut command-I (Mac) or control-I (Windows).

NOTE ! This walkthrough should give you a better understanding of how you can use mixed media types to create layer masks in your Photoshop document. If you want to use text as the basis of a mask in future, be sure to also check out the dedicated horizontal and vertical text mask options on the fly-out menu of the text tool icon.

Working with layer masks

In much the same way that you might cover up parts of a wall you are painting with masking tape so that your paint doesn't encroach into areas you want to keep clean, a layer mask will prevent your layer's contents being visible in certain areas, so that those layers below it can show through, regardless of the extent of the contents on the layer itself. Here's how you can apply one to your images. We're going to create a postcard-style mask using text.

01 Open your image and double-click the background layer to unlock it. Give it a new name. Without unlocking it, you can't apply a mask. Masks can be made using any shapes or, in this case, text, so next switch to the text tool.

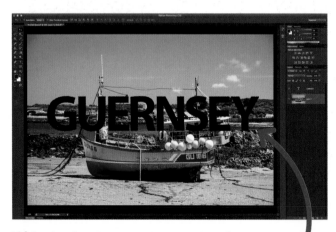

We're trying to recreate a postcard effect where the background will show through the letters, so we've used a bold font and adjusted it manually so that the letters sit closer together.

02 Whenever you create a mask and attach it to a layer, the only parts of the layer that will be totally visible are those where the mask is white. Any areas where the mask is black will be completely obscured. If you use other colours and shades on your mask, Photoshop will calculate how much of the layer to show in accordance with how bright or dark the tone is at each point. Here, we have typed in our text on a new layer on top of the background. We'll delete it in a minute but first, having finished typing, we need to switch to the Move tool and hold down the command (Mac) or control (PC) key while clicking on the thumbnail of the text in the layers palette.

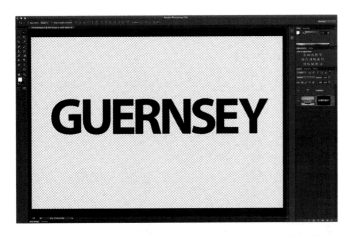

03 Clicking the text layer selected everything darker than 50% opacity – ie. just the text. The text outline is loaded as a path, which we can use as our mask on the layer below. To do that we select the background and then click the mask button. At first it looks like everything other than the text has been removed, but that's because the text layer is above the background. Our masked image is still there.

This is the Mask tool. Click here to add a blank mask to your current layer, or use the selected path to mask the image.

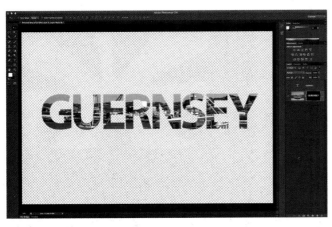

By default your layer and its mask are linked so that moving one also moves the other. Clicking this chain, however, unlinks them so that you can drag the mask without moving the image, allowing you to change what shows through.

04 We can now hide or delete the text layer as we don't need to use it any more. The result is that where the text once ran across the middle of the canvas we now have just the word GUERNSEY with the picture showing through the letters themselves. Removing the mask would reveal the rest of the image, so we haven't lost anything by blanking out part of it in this way.

The mask itself works just like any other image element, so we can use the paint brush tool, with white ink selected, to selectively paint on the mask and reveal more of the underlying image, or use black ink to block out some of the parts that are already visible. Make sure you click on the mask thumbnail before starting to avoid painting on the picture itself.

Working with blend modes

Blend modes make fundamental changes to the way that one layer changes the appearance of those that sit below it. A thorough understanding of what each blend option does will therefore enormously broaden both your options and your abilities when it comes to creating truly original, compelling compositions.

In this section we'll walk you through practical examples of every blend mode so that you can see in practice what the effect would be on your own work. Through necessity, so that it's clear what they do, we have used a very simple graphic as our base layer.

In this instance, we have typed two lines of text and used them to create a selection, which we have then filled with a simple black to grey gradient, placed on a new layer. On top of this we have added a sunburst, created using two grey tones, one of which is around 25% brightness and the other of which is around 75% brightness. We will use

the layer blend modes on this sunburst layer to effect the appearance of the text layer.

You can find the layer blend modes in the drop-down menu above the layers themselves, at the top of the Layers palette. The same options also appear on the toolbar at the top of the Photoshop interface when they can be applied to individual tools, at which point they will have the same effect as they

would have done if you had applied them layer-wide.

Note that not all of these blending mode options are available at all colour depths. Notably, several are missing when working with 32-bit images. If you need to use any that are excluded, reduce the colour depth of your image by picking wither 8bits/channel or 16bits/channel from the Image | Mode menu.

Our original images

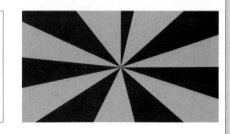

To demonstrate the effect of each blend mode, we put together these two images, with the text layer sitting below the sunburst effect in the layers stack. In each instance, the blending adjustment was applied to the sunburst graphic so that its effect could be viewed on the text layer. Opacity was left at 100% in all but one instance (detailed in the pages that follow). To accurately demonstrate the hue, saturation, colour and luminosity blend modes, colour was introduced to the sunburst graphic when using the final four blend modes. The text fill was graduated to demonstrate the different effects with difference brightness levels.

Normal Quite simply, anything in the upper layer that's not transparent obscures whatever appears in the layer below it. In our example there are no transparent pixels in the sunburst layer so you can't see the text layer below it at all.

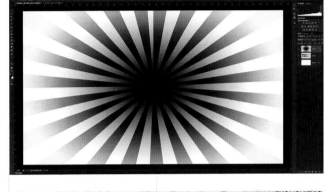

Dissolve Choose Dissolve and set a level of opacity on the drop-down menu beside the blend mode options, and Photoshop will apply a randomised dissolving effect on your upper layer that leaves the same percentage of the upper layer visible as specified in the opacity menu. Where using the opacity selector normally applies a uniform fade across the whole of the layer, though, Dissolve simply sets the specified percentage of random pixels so that they are totally transparent, while retaining the rest of the pixels at full opacity. In this example we have set the opacity to 85%, so 15% of the pixels have been removed in a random pattern to reveal the layer below.

Darken Darken only makes the layer visible on lighter parts of the layer or layers below, thus darkening them. So, in this instance we can see that it has made the sunburst visible across all of the white areas of the lower layer, and across the letters to the right of the frame, which are lighter, while the letters on the left, which are darker, are not obscured by the sunburst layer.

Multiply One step on from Darken, this multiplies together the brightness values of the layer to which it is applied with those on the visible parts of the layers below. In this example, therefore, it has darkened all of the letters on the lower layer, regardless of their own original colours.

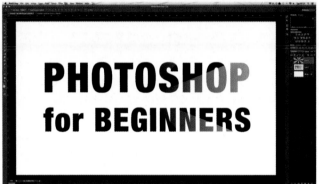

Color Burn Again, this adjustment uses the tones of the upper layer to darken the colours in the layer below by increasing the contrast, but won't apply to layers that are empty. So, where in the darken and multiply modes we could still see the whole of the sunburst pattern, regardless of whether or not it was sitting on top of a darker element on the layer below, the upper layer is effectively masked when using color burn so that it's not visible in the white or empty portions below.

Linear Burn Rather than increasing the contrast of the layer below, which is what color burn does, linear burn uses the upper layer as a guide for decreasing the brightness of the layer below. It therefore also decreases the brightness of underlying white areas, so is visible across the canvas in this example.

Darker Color Here, Photoshop compares the layer to which we are applying the blending adjustment with the visible layers below it and retains the darkest tone. So, in this example, the darker end of the words, which are darker than any part of the sunburst, take precedence. However, at the other end of the text the characters are lighter than any part of the sunburst, so both the light and dark tones of the sunburst take precedence.

Quick tip: Applying blend modes

Blend modes are selected using the drop-down menu at the top of the Layers palette. If the Layers palette isn't visible in your interface, activate it by picking from the **Window I Layers** menu, or use the keyboard shortcut **F7**.

Lighten Logically, the opposite of the Darken blend mode. The only parts of the upper layer that are visible are those that are lighter than those in the same position on the layer below. So in this example, where the left of the text is black it is obviously darker than all tones in the sunburst, so the sunburst is visible within the characters there. However, on the right, the text is lighter than any tone in the sunburst, so none of the sunburst is visible. The sunburst isn't visible on the background, either, since it's white or transparent.

Screen Effectively works out how much brighter than pure black the upper layer is, and uses this to increase the brightness of the layer below it by the same amount. If the upper layer is black, the underlying colour will be unchanged since there is no difference to be calculated. If the upper layer is white, then the difference between this and black is 100%, so the brightness of the underlying layer will be increased by 100% to produce white on that underlying layer, too.

Color Dodge Lightens the contents of the layers below with reference to the upper layer by decreasing the contrast. In our example, therefore, Where the light parts of the sunburst lay on top of the text, the lighter parts of the text are lost as the contrast between them and their surroundings is reduced to virtually nothing.

Linear Dodge (Add) Brightens the underlying layer to reflect the brightness of the layer to which we have applied the blending adjustment. If any portion of the upper layer is black it will not make any difference to the brightness of the underlying layer. Here, no parts of the sunburst are black, so everything on the underlaying text layer has been lightened, with those parts that fall under the brighter portions of the sunburst brightened the most.

Vivid Light Another variation on the two lighting effects above, this one instead uses burning on darker tones and dodging on lighter ones to adjust colours. Burning is a technique used by traditional photographers to expose the sensitive paper for longer so that the result is darker, whereas dodging exposes the paper for a shorter amount of time, often by obscuring the fall of the light, to expose it less, and thus allow more of the paper's original colour – white – to show through.

Overlay Mixes together the colours in the top layer with the visible colours below it to determine the overall brightness of the visible layers below it. So, for those parts of the top layer where the brightness is between 51% and 100% (mid-grey to white in our case) the underlying layer will be made brighter. Where the upper later is between 0% and 49% brightness (black to mid-grey in this case) the underlying layer will be made darker. Where the brightness of the upper layer sits exactly half way through the luminosity spectrum – at 50% – no change will be made to the brightness of those parts of the layers below it.

Soft Light Adobe likens this to shining a diffused spotlight on the canvas. If the colour of the top layer is lighter than 50% of the maximum possible brightness, the image below is lightened, and vice versa.

Hard Light Where soft light affects the underlying colours by darkening or lightening them, hard light multiplies or screens them. As you'll remember from the explanations above, multiply darkens tones by multiplying together the brightness values of the darker tones, while screen lightens brighter tones by increasing its brightness by the percentage by which the adjusted layer is brighter than mid-grey.

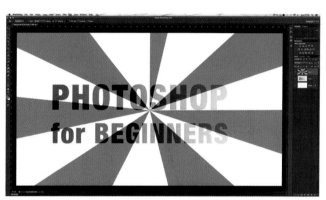

Lighter Color Quite logically, this is the opposite of the Darker Color blend mode. It looks at the layer to which it is applied and compares it to what is visible below it and keeps the brighter pixels in each instance. This has therefore made a difference to the appearance of the darker end of our text, since the sunburst is lighter than it, but no difference to the lighter end of our text as it is lighter than the sunburst.

Linear Light Uses changes in contrast as a means of darkening or lightening parts of the underlaying layer, boosting the contrast on those areas where the contents of the upper layer are closer to black than white, and brightening those where it's closer to white than black.

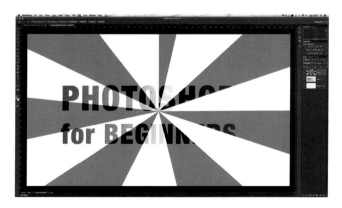

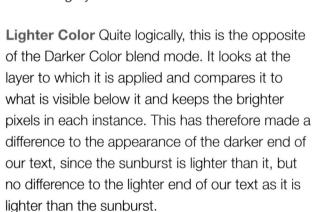

Pin Light Replaces the brightest parts of the adjusted layer with any that are darker than it in the visible layers below, while replacing the darkest pixels in the adjusted layer with those that are lighter than it in the visible parts of the layers below.

Hard Mix Works in a slightly different manner depending on whether you are working with a red, green, blue (RGB) image, or cyan, magenta, yellow, black (CMYK). In either case it adds the primary tones (RGB or CMYK) of the adjusted layer to those of the layers below to work out what colour to produce. If the result of the additions is more than the maximum value for each colour, it resorts to just using the maximum colour in each instance.

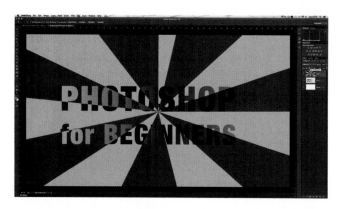

Difference Subtracts the colour from the adjusted layer if the colour on the layers below is darker, and vice versa. Black is considered to have no colour since it is completely dark, so black areas on your adjusted layer won't affect the appearance of your document at all. White, on the other hand, is made from 100% colour on all channels in RGB images, so inverts the underlying layers where it appears on the adjusted layer.

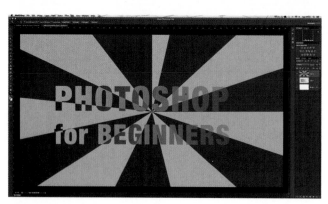

Exclusion Exclusion simultaneously applies the adjustment we saw in Difference, above, and uses the brightness of the adjusted layer as a guide for masking the result, so very dark parts of the adjusted layer will make very little difference to the appearance of the layer below.

Subtract Photoshop first takes the value of the colour for each channel (RGB or CMYK) in the adjusted layer, then the same values from the underlying area, and subtracts the first from the second. If the first is greater than the second, it stops at zero rather than stepping into negative figures, which would result in an absence of that particular colour in that part of the image.

Divide The methodology here is similar to that for the subtract adjustment, but rather than taking one value from the other it divides the colour values for each part of the underlying layer by the colour values of each part of the layer above.

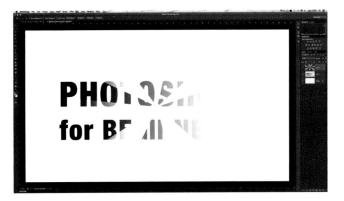

Hue Swaps out the hue of the underlying image with the hue of the adjusted layer, but retains the luminance and saturation of the original layer that sits underneath it. Note that for the sake of these last four examples – hue, saturation, color, luminosity – we have changed the colour of the sunburst effect in our composition.

Saturation Similar to the Hue adjustment, Saturation retains only the saturation values of the blended upper layer and applies them to the underlying layers while retaining the underlying layers' hue and luminance values.

Color Retains only the luminance of the layers below but replaces all of their colour with the colour, hue and saturation of the blended layer above. In Adobe's own words, because this doesn't change the lighting of the layer below it's useful when colouring old monochrome images.

Luminosity Applies the luminance levels of each part of the blended layer to the layers below it while retaining their hue and saturation values. As can be seen from the example here, it is often necessary to reduce the opacity of the layer to view its effect on the layers below. Here we have reduced it to 75%.

Still confused?

The simplest way to think about blend modes is to concentrate on one word: 'blend'. Quite simply, they blend with the layer below them, and in doing so make a fundamental change to that layer, possibly even sacrificing their own appearance in the composition entirely as they disappear according to the relative strengths of their own tones and those with which they're reacting.

You can only apply one blend mode to any single layer, but you can stack several identical layers on top of one another and apply a different blend mode to each one, bearing in mind that if it interacts with the result of an existing blend below it, the result may be different to what you expected.

Be careful not to confuse blend modes with adjustment layers, which can have equally dramatic effects, as we'll explore next.

Using Adjustment Layers and layer fills

For a long time, you could only populate your Layers with pixels or vector graphics. That all changed with the arrival of adjustment layers.

As their name suggests, adjustment layers 'adjust' the content that appears below them in the layer stack. That sounds very much like what blend modes do. However, whereas blend modes use the colour and luminance values of one layer to change the colours, luminance, saturation, hue or visibility of what appears in the visible parts of the layer stack, adjustment layers apply conventional adjustments, like those found on the Image | Adjustments menu. In this respect they don't 'blend' with the layer below, but they do act like a lens through which you can see it.

Indeed, every adjustment you can find in that menu from Brightness/Contrast down to Selective Color can be applied as a layer rather than in the conventional menu-selected manner.

Why apply filters this way?

The answer is quite simple: flexibility. When you apply a filter in the conventional manner, from the Adjustments menu, it is applied across the whole of your image at maximum strength. It is also applied in a destructive form, in that unless you step back through the history list it applies an irrevocable change to the state of the image at that point, which you'll have to work with – or around – for the rest of your editing session.

Layer fills

The same menu through which we access the adjustment layers also gives us easy access to a selection of layer fills, which are replicated in the conventional Layer | New Fill Layer menu.

Any new layer created in this manner can be filled with a colour, gradient or pattern.

The incentive to add new layers of these types through the Layers palette is broadly one of convenience, since

Adjustments and fills

Adjustment layers and fill layers are both applied by clicking the semi-filled circle at the bottom of the Layers palette. Each of the options you'll find here are replicated elsewhere in the Photoshop main menus, but by applying them as a layer you'll retain better control as they can be tweaked using opacity controls and masks.

adding them through the regular menu also attaches a layer mask – as this method does – and retains the ability to control its appearance using the opacity slider.

Using opacity to control an adjustment layer

01 Here we have a fairly ordinary picture. The composition is respectable enough and there's nothing wrong with the subject matter, but the overall photo lacks punch, largely because of the washed out colours in the sky. We can improve it enormously by applying the channel mixer on an adjustment layer.

02 The Channel Mixer lets us adjust the individual levels of red, green and blue in our image, and supplements the sliders for these with a fourth one covering contrast. In this instance we've dragged the blue slider to the left to give the sky a bit more punch and also pulled back a little on the reds to darken them off.

Selectively applying adjustment layers with masks

01 Rather than using the colour mixer we have addressed the issue of our insipid sky by using the hue and saturation sliders this time around. We have increased the level of saturation enormously to really strengthen the colours in the image, pushed the hue slightly and applied a very small negative adjustment to the level of lightness. However, because we aren't addressing individual colour channels each of these adjustments has been applied to the whole of the image, including the yellow wheat stubble, which we don't want to change in this instance.

03 Those changes made a big difference, but as you can see from the live preview behind the Channel Mixer panel in step 2 the sky is now too blue to look realistic. With our new adjustment layer selected we can therefore use the opacity slider to dial down the strength of the adjustment until it's more believable.

04 And here's the difference we have made. Without using any brushes or making any permanent changes to our canvas through the Adjustments menu we have boosted the blue in the sky. If we later decide that it's too much we can either tweak the opacity again, remove the adjustment layer or use a mask to control it.

02 Obviously we want to remove this adjustment from the stubble, so we will apply a layer mask to the adjustment layer in just the same way as we would apply a mask to a regular pixel-based layer. You'll notice from the Layers palette in the grab for step 1 that there is already a mask attached to our adjustment layer. At the moment it's empty meaning that the adjustment applies across the whole canvas. In step 2, we have therefore applied a black-to-white gradient fill, with black at the bottom and white at the top, to block the adjustment from touching the wheat.

Layer styles

As you should have realised by now, Layers are one of the most important tools at your disposal when working in Photoshop. Not only do they help you work in a more organised manner by arranging the different parts of your composition across different discrete documents areas, tied up in a single unified project, but they also let you apply adjustments and make changes in a non-destructive manner.

The last aspect we'll look at in our exploration of the power of layers is Layer Styles. These constitute a series of additional attributes that you can append to existing layers to change how they appear within the stack, and include such common add-ons as drop shadows, inner glows, bevels and embossing. Many are most impressive – and most useful – when applied to text.

In this section we'll walk you through the process of using layer effects to achieve a variety of creative, original outcomes in your daily work.

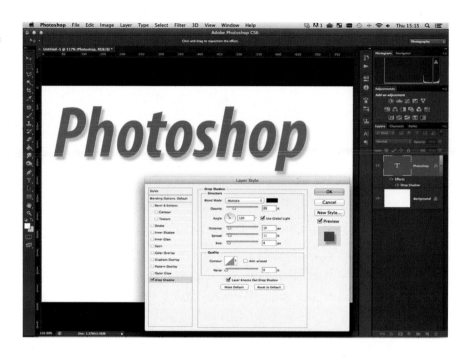

Applying your first layer style

The Layer Styles control sits at the bottom of the Layers panel (see below right). This contains direct links to each of the available effects. Selecting one opens the full Layer Styles palette (see above) through which you can apply different amendments to the currently-selected layer.

The majority of these styles work with virtual light. Drop shadow, which we are applying in the grab above, for example, casts a copy of the current

layer's contents behind the original. By sliding the opacity control left and right you can respectively lighten and strengthen the result. Other controls let you change the colour of the shadow and even

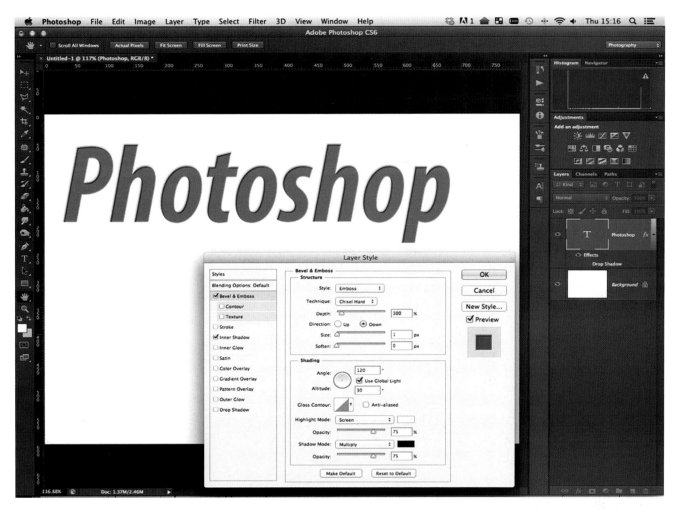

the angle from which the light is striking it.

Sometimes you'll need to apply more than one style to your content to achieve the result you are after – or at least to heighten the sense of realism you're after.

In the above example we have deactivated the drop shadow but have applied both an emboss using the panel of the panel that is currently visible, and an inner shadow. Both of these sit within the

bounds of the selected text and make it look like it is pressed down into the canvas.

You'll notice that although we have disabled the drop shadow by clearing the check box beside its entry in the Layer Styles sidebar it still remains in the Layers panel, inset beneath the layer of text to which it was applied. However, we can see at a glance that it's not active, even when we close the Layer Styles panel, because it doesn't have a picture of an eye beside

it, which is used against all layers and layer styles that are present in the document.

You can control layer styles in just the same way as you would any other style, dragging them from one layer to another or dropping them onto the trash icon.

You can't duplicate them by dragging them onto the new icon at the bottom of the Layers palette, but you can copy them by right-clicking and paste the copy onto other layers.

Chapter 4
Saving and printing

With your work now complete, it's time to hit save
and think about how it's going to be used.

•

Photoshop can read and write an impressive range
of file types, but some are more appropriate than
others. Here we'll show you how to pick the best
format for your work according to its intended use.
We'll walk you through the process of compressing
your work for the web without having a noticeably
detrimental impact on its appearance, and
we'll identify the most important settings in
Photoshop's extensive printing controls.

Saving your work

By now you should have a good understanding of what each tool in Photoshop can do for you and how you can put them to best use. You will also know how each one can be tweaked and its settings adjusted to suit your exact requirements. You'll have a thorough understanding of layers and how they can be used to split up the various parts of your document so that it's easy to change the prominence of some, knock back others, adjust the way they blend with one another and change their stacking order so that some sit behind others. You should know how to pick colours, how to adjust brushes and text and how to make selections. In short you should have all the knowledge you need to set out and create some great work in Photoshop.

The most important part of creating any work other than getting over the psychological stumbling block of the blank canvas is, of course, saving it. Without saving regularly you run the risk of losing it all together and without saving it at the end all of your work will be wasted.

In this last section, therefore, we shall look at saving your work both in native formats and for the web, before moving on to examine various output options such as web publishing and printing.

Saving options

As with all of the underlying options that fundamentally change the way that Photoshop works, the file saving settings are found in the preferences panel. On the Mac click Photoshop | Preferences... | File saving. On the PC pick Edit | Preferences... | File saving.

Here you'll find all of the tools you need to change the way Photoshop handles outputting your files to disk. As with all settings dialogues it's best to work from the top to the bottom, picking the options you want in each case. We would recommend that you leave as many of the defaults in place as

possible since they are set up to keep your files safe. However, there are some things you can do to speed things up and save space.

If you're using Photoshop CS6 you can now opt to have files saved in the background while you carry on working. This is a significant time saver since it doesn't interrupt your workflow. You should therefore ensure that the Save in Background option is checked. Also make sure you are happy with the interval at which recovery information is saved. By default this is set to 10 minutes, but can be reduced to 5 minutes if you want to be ultra-careful or extended as far as one hour if you are confident that your machine is stable and you are happy to run the risk of losing an hour's worth of work if it crashes (see grab, opposite). We would recommend being more cautious than Adobe suggests here by trimming the save interval to five minutes.

Some settings can be adjusted or disabled simply to save them from nagging

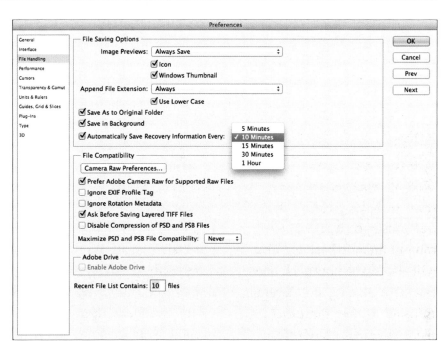

» *Think carefully about how often you want Photoshop to save recovery information to reduce the risk you'll lose precious work.*

you. For example, by default Photoshop will check whether you really do want to save layered Tiff files. These consume considerable space and so you might want to flatten them before saving. By checking each time, Photoshop is effectively offering to save you some space. Saving layered Tiff files can be useful since they can make use of alpha channels which are used to define which parts of the image should remain transparent, and by flattening the image you will naturally lose this data.

Tiff is a very widely accepted format, but it's not the best one to use for saving work you'll will want to edit in the future. For that you should use native Photoshop formats. You can therefore treat Tiff as a destination format that you will use to output your work once you've finished it. Layers will therefore be less important in the finished document, and so leaving this option checked is a useful reminder that you should flatten your image before saving it to save

on space and so that it opens more quickly the next time it is accessed. However, once you have flattened the image, which you can do from the layers menu, don't forget to undo the action if you want to save it again as a Photoshop document or you'll lose all of your layers.

Maximising compatibility

The last option in the file compatibility box is whether or not to maximise compatibility with PSD and PSB files. PSD is the default Photoshop document format. It can be a maximum of 2GB in size and no more than 30,000 pixels

tall or wide. PSB stands for Photoshop big, and is used to save documents up to 10 times that size in either direction and four terabytes on disc.

Both formats are very similar and well documented, so many third-party applications can also open them. New versions of Photoshop can almost always access documents saved in older versions, and in some cases older versions can open files created in later editions. This makes PSD and PSB file formats fairly safe as containers for your work.

However, over time things will inevitably change and you can't absolutely guarantee that the work you create today will be accessible in five, 10 or more years time if you don't still have access to today's version of Photoshop (which might not run on a later operating system). Likewise, if you try to share your work with other people, perhaps because you're designing a graphic for the cover of a book or a flyer and need to send it to a print shop or designer, you can't be totally sure that all of your layers, adjustments, blending settings and so on will be rendered in their version of Photoshop in exactly the same manner unless they are using the same version with the same plug-ins, fonts, colour settings and so on.

Photoshop tries to cater for this possibility by offering to maximise compatibility in native PSD and PSB files, and the first time you save your work in one of these formats it will pop up a dialogue asking whether or not you like to maximise compatibility. It will remember whether you chose yes or no and will not ask you again where that file

What is maximising compatibility?

Because no version of Photoshop can know which edition of the application will be used to open the file that you save, it can't guarantee that all the features you have used will be supported. Therefore, to reduce the likelihood that the document will be completely incomprehensible when opened in earlier versions or third-party applications with incomplete conformity, the Maximise Compatibility command saves a flattened composite version of your work alongside the fully layered edition.

Anyone who is using an application that needs to resort to the composite edition will lose a lot of the editing options open to those who can read all of the layers, and if they go on to save the document again much of the data will be lost, but at least it means they'll be able to see what you've done and, if they're acting in a purely editorial role, sign it off.

While enabling this option would therefore seem to be a smart move it's not without its costs. Saving a flattened version alongside your layered file takes time, and so slows down the saving process. It also takes space, so your files will be larger, which not only means that they'll take longer to open but they also occupy more of your drive space and will take longer to email. Careful thought therefore needs to be given to whether or not you want to maximise compatibility (which would be our recommendation) or save on time and space.

Fortunately, with Photoshop CS6 now able to save in the background, the delay in saving with this option enabled is reduced since you can continue working while it writes to disk, but you'll still incur the time penalty when it comes to opening compatible files in the first place.

is concerned, but the next time you save a different Photoshop document the dialogue will pop up once more. This can become tiring, so you can disable it from the preferences panel by picking Never or set Photoshop to always maximise compatibility. Either way, you won't be asked in future whether or not this is something you would like it to do. The result is less frustration and more saved time.

File formats

The simplest manner in which to save your file is to use the shortcut ctrl-S on the PC or command-S on the Mac. If you haven't already saved the file at least once this will call up the Save As dialogue, which you can access later using ctrl-shift-S on PC or command-shift-S on the Mac.

Either of these shortcuts calls up the regular file management dialogue for either Windows or Mac, depending on your platform, with a box at the top for the filename, a button to create new folders below and, in between, a view of your existing files and a series of controls for choosing the format to use for the current file.

If you are saving work that's incomplete or which you want to share with other Photoshop users then naturally it makes sense to use the Photoshop format, which will likely be the default selection on the Format drop-down menu (see below). However, this is just one of many different formats that Photoshop can read and

» *The file save dialogue pops up the first time you save your work, and can be accessed in future by using Save As on the file menu, or any of the available keyboard shortcuts. It uses the standard OS layout.*

write, and the full list will change depending on the colour depth of your image. Not all file formats can save the full range of colours open to designers and so those options will disappear from the format menu when you start to use 16- or 32-bit colour depths.

If the format you need to use isn't on the list then click Cancel to exit the dialogue and pick Image | Mode | 8-bits/ channel to reduce the colour depth of your image, then try saving the file again. If the file was originally in 16- or 32-bit colour you should now see

a wider range of formats to choose from, and the one you need will likely be available.

Some of the options open to you when saving your file will be determined by the make up of your document. For example, if you have only used one layer, perhaps because all you've been doing is colour-correcting a photo, then the option to save layers will naturally be irrelevant, and so will be greyed out. Likewise, if you're not using a file format that supports transparency then the Alpha Channels option will be greyed out. In general, you

don't need to worry about any of the greyed out options unless they are specifically required in your current project. If that's the case then it indicates that you have chosen an inappropriate file format and should choose an alternative from the format menu.

One option that will always be available is the 'As a Copy' feature. This lets you save a new version of your file in a separate document without using the Save As option. You might want to do this if you're planning on performing some radical edits to your document that may do some harm or will be significantly different to the original and you want to keep multiple versions so that, for example, you can allow a client to choose between them or you can compare them later to see which you prefer without running the risk of damaging your original assets.

```
✓ Photoshop
  Large Document Format
  Perfect Resize Format
  BMP
  CompuServe GIF
  Dicom
  Photoshop EPS
  IFF Format
  JPEG
  JPEG 2000
  JPEG Stereo
  Multi-Picture Format
  PCX
  Photoshop PDF
  Photoshop 2.0
  Photoshop Raw
  Pixar
  PNG
  Portable Bit Map
  Scitex CT
  Targa
  TIFF
  Photoshop DCS 1.0
  Photoshop DCS 2.0
```

```
✓ Photoshop
  Large Document Format
  Perfect Resize Format
  Cineon
  Dicom
  IFF Format
  JPEG
  JPEG 2000
  JPEG Stereo
  Multi-Picture Format
  Photoshop PDF
  Photoshop Raw
  PNG
  Portable Bit Map
  TIFF
```

» *The range of file formats in which Photoshop can save varies depending on the colour depth of your image with 8-bit images compatible with a wider range of formats (left) than 16-bit (above) or 32-bit files.*

Optimising images for use on the web

Several years ago Adobe produced a companion application called Image Ready that was used specifically to reduce the size of files so that they were more appropriate for use on the web. At the same time its major competitor, Macromedia, which it has since acquired, produced a rival application called

Fireworks. Fireworks still exists as part of Creative Suite and over time its focus has changed slightly to encompass a more universal web content creation workflow.

Image Ready, on the other hand, disappeared a while back and its features were rolled into Photoshop itself. Now it's no longer necessary to reopen

your work in a second tool to format it for use on the web; you can do that directly within the application in which it was created.

Save for web

The tool that does this is called, quite logically, Save for Web and you'll find it on the File

» *The best starting point when saving images for the web is to use one of the presets on the drop-down menu, with JPEG, GIF and PNG all suitable starting points for general web use.*

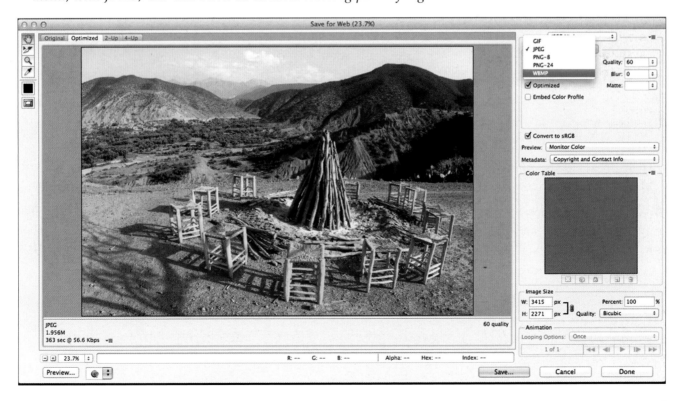

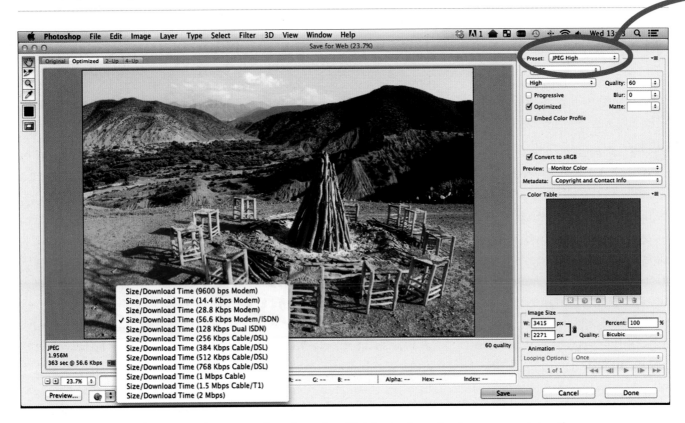

» *The menu below the image shows you how long it will take to download over a variety of common connection types. Try to keep the result as low as possible for a nimble, responsive site.*

menu or by pressing shift-control-alt-S on the PC or shift-command-alt-S on the Mac.

At its most basic it allows you to reduce the file size of your image using a range of presets for JPEGs, GIFs and PNG files, and your choice of format will be determined largely by the content of your document.

Photos, for example, are usually best served by the JPEG format. Business and vector graphics, on the other hand, are more suited to being saved as GIF or PNG files, as you can see from the example images on the opposite page where the more efficiently-compressed image on the left is quite mucky, while the less compressed one to the right is fairly clean. The one to the right might therefore represent your brand values more effectively, but it would take a long time to download, thus slowing down your site and undoing any of the good you have done by keeping your production quality high, as your visitors may give up waiting for the data to appear and look elsewhere.

Save for Web interface

You can select a preset using the Preset control at the top of the Save for Web dialogue or using the drop-down menu below it to pick a file format. Using this secondary file format menu also gives you the option of saving as a WBMP file, which was a popular format for use in the early days of mobile phone Internet access.

The Save for Web interface is designed to make it easy for you to see what effect your changes will have on the

You can save time and get started quickly by picking a preset from the drop-down menu at the top of the sidebar

quality of your image, as any form of compression for web use inevitably requires that certain data is removed from your image to make is smaller. This can manifest itself as noise along sharp contrasts in a JPEG file (see below) or a reduction in the number of colours in a GIF file. Successfully re-purposing your image for use on the web requires that you minimise the impact of your actions wherever possible while simultaneously making the biggest difference to the file size.

At the top of the main part of the interface you will therefore see four tabs marked Original, Optimised, 2-Up and 4-Up. Click Original and you'll see your image in its current state without any compression applied. Click Optimised and you'll switch to what it looks like with the settings selected in the right-hand sidebar applied. With any luck you won't see too much difference between the two, but take a look at the file size information below the image. This is an indication of how much space your image will consume on the server once uploaded to your website, and will also give you an idea of how long it will take to download. The line below it

» *Both of the images below have been compressed as JPEGs. However, the one on the left has been heavily compressed to produce a smaller file size while the one on the right has been lightly compressed. The difference is clear, with a noticeably dirtier result in the left hand image.*

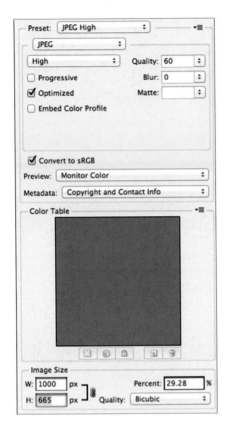

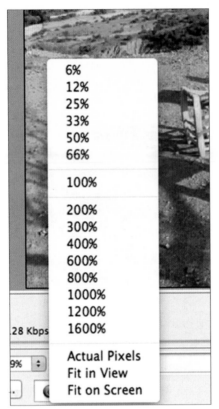

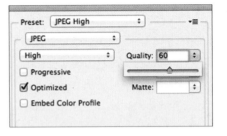

» *When working with JPEGs, start by reducing the quality level to increase compression.*

image is therefore going to take, say, 10 seconds to download it's probably too large and you should use the options in the right-hand sidebar to reduce its size and thus the amount of time it will take to download.

While doing this you can either click backwards and forwards between the Original and Optimised tabs or click 2-Up or 4-Up to show the original and various compression options side-by-side. This makes it easier to choose the best treatment for your work.

Note that if using the four-up view you can keep the original image on screen alongside up to three other versions with different optimisation settings.

» *There's no point saving a file that's physically larger than it needs to be, so reduce its dimensions before you start.*

balances download time with connection speed. You'll notice that there is a drop-down menu to the right, which you call up by clicking the icon at the end of this line, which lets you select from a range of different connection speeds to see how long a user on a connection of

» *Always preview your images at a size that lets you see how they are being degraded clearly in the optimise tab panel.*

that type would expect to wait for your image to appear (see the grab on page 122).

Bear in mind when working with Save for Web that most Internet users are fairly impatient and don't want to wait more than a few seconds for a page to load. If your

» *The image at the top contains 256 colours; the one below it contains just 32. Although you can see that there is some speckling in the section of the 32-colour image zoomed to 100% that isn't evident in the first one, the result is still pretty good as dithering is set to 100%.*

Compressing your image for use on the web

Start by selecting a file format from the top of the sidebar, then skip straight down to the bottom of the sidebar and set your image dimensions. There's no point in saving a photo at its full size if it's ever going to be 400 or 500 pixels wide when used on the web since it will take a long time to download only to be resized in situ. Resize it in advance and not only will your site be more responsive, but you'll also have greater control over the result.

If you can't say for sure right now how large the image will be once it's incorporated into your website then make an educated guess. It's unlikely that many images will be used at more than 1000 pixels wide as beyond this point you risk it is not fitting within a tablet display without being reduced in size. A width of 1000 pixels is therefore fairly good starting point and unless you have a specific reason to choose something else.

Notice how the width and height boxes are joined together with a chain icon to their right. This indicates that they are linked and that in order to maintain the proper proportions of your image Photoshop will automatically adjust the width if you enter the height manually or the height if you have entered the width so that the shape of the original is reflected in the shape of the optimised document. If you don't want to maintain the original proportions and instead would rather specify both a height and width manually, click the chain icon to unlink the two boxes.

If changing the size of the image has made it too small for you to view with any great detail in the preview window then use the magnification control in the bottom left-hand corner to enlarge it

either to 100% or to fit within the view (ie the Save for Web window) before continuing. It's important that you are able to see clearly what affect you are having on your image while making changes so that you know how it will appear on the web.

Performing the compression

Now turn your attention back to the top of the sidebar. The precise options open to you will vary depending on the file format you have chosen for your optimised image. Choose JPEG, for example, and you can set the quality level using a sliding scale or choose a preset from the drop-down menu.

The higher the number you choose on the scale, the less obvious your compression will be but, at the same time, you will also save less space.

By reducing the quality level considerably you can save an enormous amount of space when using JPEG but you will also degrade the quality of the image and this degradation will

be most obvious along sharp contrasts which is why JPEG is less suitable for use when compressing text or graphics with flat colours and sharp edges such as charts, titles, headlines and so on.

If you've chosen to compress your image using the GIF format you will instead compress the image by reducing the number of colours. For the most faithful reproduction of your original you would choose 256 colours, but again this would do little to reduce your file size, so for the greatest effectiveness you would click on the double headed arrow at the end of the Colours box and choose one of the precepts or type your own value into the box.

As you do, see what effect it has on the previewed image. If you reduce it too much you will notice that the image becomes grainy, but by carefully balancing the number of colours you can make a significant file size saving. You can also help by making sure that the amount of dither

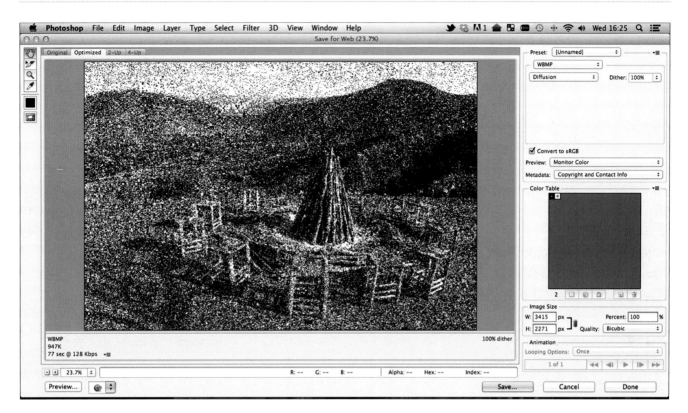

in the box below your chosen number of colours is high so that the colours are distributed in a manner that reduces the obviousness of your compression activities.

The workflows for GIF and PNG-8 are very closely related where compression is concerned and so it makes sense to switch between these two in the sidebar as you work on compressing your graphics so that you can see whether one offers slightly better quality and a slightly smaller resulting file than the other.

GIF and PNG also both support transparency which will allow you to create

seemingly irregular shaped graphics for use on your site. Any areas that are transparent in the original image can also be set to remain transparent within the optimised file so if, say, you had used a particular font for a title on your website and saved it as a graphic because you knew you couldn't use it as a font for the type on your site, you could position this on top of a coloured, patterned or photographic background on your site if you selected GIF or PNG format and made sure that the transparency box was ticked. The background would then show up between the letters.

Unless you have a very specific reason for using it you should steer clear of WBMP as the result is a very scratchy black and white dithered image, as you can see above.

Once you have reduced the image to a reasonable size, click Save... and Photoshop will ask you to supply a new name. If you have previously saved an optimised version of the file as try to save this one over the top it will allow you to do so, but will warn you in advance so that you don't undo any good work you have performed already. You can now upload the optimised image to your server for use on your website.

Printing your work

When you've finished creating your work you won't always want to upload it to the web; often you'll want to create a hard copy. The best way to do this is usually to send it to a professional online printing service as they can usually guarantee the best quality output at a reasonable price in a fairly short amount of time. However, if you own a good inkjet printer or you just want to produce a quick and cheap proof print then you'll want to output it yourself at home.

Photoshop's built-in printing tools are just as accomplished as its editing tools. You'll find them on the File menu. However, there are a little more complicated to use than the printing controls you would come across in your word processor or spreadsheet app.

If you only have one printer attached to your computer or on your network and with the necessary drivers installed then this will automatically appear at the top of the sidebar. If you have several, use the drop-down menu to pick the one to which you want to send

» *Photoshop's printing controls are highly accomplished and contain far more options than the print dialogue you'll have come across in a regular productivity application.*

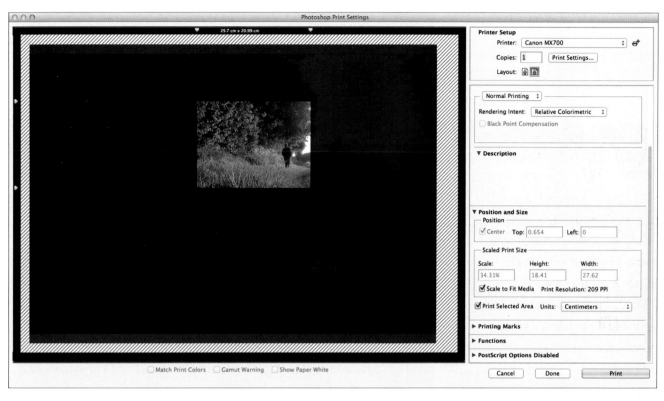

» *If you only want to print a section of your canvas, select it using the marquee tool and then pick the Print Selected Area option in the dialogue. The handles in the margins let you tailor the precise printed area.*

your image. Clicking the Print settings... button opens up the regular printer controls for that device, but most of the controls you need to use to tailor the appearance of your output are contained within the sidebar.

The main part of the printer dialogue is consumed by a preview of your image showing how it will appear on the page. There's a good chance that it will be too large to fit onto your selected paper. The size of your image is determined by the resolution and number of pixels per inch you specified

when setting up the canvas in the first place. However, you can change its placement on the page from this dialogue. Further down the sidebar you will see a box marked Scaled Print Size, inside of which are controls for scale as a percentage of the original image and specific height and width measurements. You can also check the box to automatically scale your image to fit on the page, which is often the best move.

Keep an eye on the print resolution, which is displayed

just below the height and width boxes and shows you how many pixels will appear within each horizontal or vertical inch of the printed image at your currently specified dimensions. You should aim to keep this above 150ppi wherever possible as below this level it is often possible to make out the individual dots themselves using the naked eye from average reading distances.

Sometimes you won't want to print the whole of an image. In such instances you can use the regular marquee tool in the

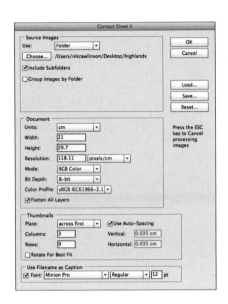

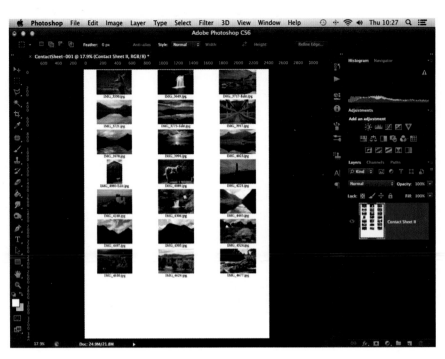

» *The Contact Sheet II settings (above left) let you specify the layout of a page of thumbnails (above right) which can be sent to a client for approval, saving you the expense of printing each one full size.*

Photoshop editing environment to select the area you want to print and then, in the print dialogue, check the box beside Print Selected Area. Having done this you will see the selected area highlighted within the print preview with the rest of the image dimmed. You can drag the handles in the top and left margins to change the size of the selected print area on the page and use the Scale setting to enlarge it.

When you have set all the options to meet your requirements click the Print button to output the image to your device.

Creating a contact sheet

If you are using Photoshop in a professional capacity to edit images you've shot for a client then it isn't practical (and often too expensive) to print every image this way for their approval. It is more usual, therefore, to print what is known as a contact sheet, which is made up of thumbnails of each image from the shoot from which the client can select the ones they want to see full-size.

Years ago it would have been necessary to lay out these images in a desktop publishing application or to compose a

montage within Photoshop itself. However, for several years Photoshop been able to automate the process of building a contact sheet.

Organise your images into a dedicated folder and then pick File | Automate | Contact Sheet II. Use the various settings to define how you would like the sheet to be laid out and Photoshop will automatically create a collage of the chosen images with their filenames below each one. You can now print this and send it to your client, allowing them to choose the images they would like you to print full size.